Theodore Whitefield Hunt

American Meditative Lyrics

Theodore Whitefield Hunt

American Meditative Lyrics

ISBN/EAN: 9783744795609

Printed in Europe, USA, Canada, Australia, Japan

Cover: Foto ©Thomas Meinert / pixelio.de

More available books at **www.hansebooks.com**

AMERICAN
MEDITATIVE LYRICS

BY

THEODORE W. HUNT, Ph. D., Litt. D.

PROFESSOR OF ENGLISH IN THE COLLEGE OF NEW JERSEY,
AUTHOR OF "ENGLISH PROSE AND PROSE WRITERS," ETHICAL
STUDIES IN OLD ENGLISH AUTHORS, ETC.

Illustrated

NEW YORK

E. B. TREAT, 5 COOPER UNION

OFFICE OF THE TREASURY MAGAZINE

1896

TO

EDMUND CLARENCE STEDMAN

TABLE OF CONTENTS.

PREFACE.

As indicated by the title, it is the purpose of this volume briefly to discuss American Lyrical Verse, with exclusive reference to its meditative quality as distinct from any other features it may present in the line of a more objective and secular type of poetry. Reference will be made to representative poets only—to those only whose work is specifically literary, and mainly to authors whose poetic product has already passed into literary history. No attempt will be made fully to compass so wide and fruitful a field, but only to give a view sufficiently comprehensive to meet the demands of intelligent readers, and stimulate their study along similar lines. Naturally adapted as a topic to the needs and tastes of the clergy and of those who are specially inclined or committed to the contemplative life, it is hoped that the treatise, in its simple method, may commend itself to all those who are seeking in the poetry that they read the spontaneous and serious utterances of the human heart.

T. W. H.

Princeton, N. J.,

ETRY.

11

CHAPTER FIRST.

THE SPIRITUAL ELEMENT IN POETRY.

A QUESTION of interest emerges at the outset as to the spiritual element in poetry : what it is in its essential nature, to what degree it manifests itself, what are the various forms of its manifestation, and what the characteristics and salient features which it gives to verse.   It is to this particular element in literature that Professor Corson refers, as he writes, in his " Introduction to Browning," of " the spiritual ebb and flow of verse," emphasizing the fact that it appears and recedes with something like the regularity of the tides, sometimes, at the flood, and, sometimes, at the lowest ebb.   Matthew Arnold acknowledges the presence and potency of this element, as he speaks of the Hebraic order of British verse as contrasted with the Hellenic.

13

Modern critics speak of a school of English poetry as the Oriental or scriptural, in the light of this spiritual feature, "from which source arises," says Devey, "that earnestness of purpose, that profound reflection and purity of feeling, which make the higher order of English poets . stand out in advantageous contrast to the heathen bards of antiquity." To the same effect, a living American critic, Mabie, suggestively writes: "The spiritual world is the background of almost all modern poetry, from those early songs of Longfellow, which have become the familiar psalms of universal experience, to such noble interpretations of human life from the spiritual side as Tennyson's 'In Memo iam,'" and, by way of special reference to our own verse, he adds that this particular characteristic has been illustrated, with one or two exceptions, "in the entire company of American poets." One of the marked exceptions to this principle, the poet Whitman, confirms the correctness of the statement by the severe character of the criticism to which, by way of contrast, he has voluntarily subjected himself.

Even though at times this unworldly feature has taken an unattractive and extreme form, in

the phase of a Puritan order of piety and life,
its essential basis of spirituality has been present
to give solidity and tone to literary art. Because of the fact, moreover, that in the poetry
of Poe we have an expression of moral character that is abnormal, this is not to lead us
to argue against the healthy presence of such
a quality. What, indeed, could more fully and
accurately portray the essential presence of
spiritual life, midway between the morbid verse
of Poe and the ultra-moralistic verse of Tupper,
than such sane and wholesome and meditative
lines as we find in the instructive pages of Bryant and Emerson and Longfellow and Whittier! Indeed, we go not beyond the truth of
the matter when we say that the primal function of verse, as distinct from prose, is to reveal
the supersensual to men. If Arnold is right in
saying that " the grand power of poetry is its
interpretative power," then we may add that its
main office as interpretative is to detect and disclose the spiritual element that there is in God
and nature and man and truth. It is its high
office to make the " vision divine " visible and
real to men, and so to minimize the distance between earth and heaven as to hallow the one by

the other. Hence, poetry in its origin is more divine than human, as the poets of old were poets and priests in one, composing and singing what they sang as the prophets of God for the holiest ends. " All truth," says one, " that awakens within us the feeling of the infinite is poetic." Even Byron conceived of it " as the feeling of past worlds and future," while, in the eye of such a bard as Milton or Wordsworth or Mrs. Browning or Mrs. Stowe, it never descended below the level of a specifically spiritual art. If this be so as to poetry in general, what may not be said of the high spiritual purport of lyric poetry—the utterance of the heart more than of the head, the accepted medium, in all ages and nations, for the revelation of the inner soul of man, the literary *Via Sacra*, over whose highway there pass the purest spirits of the race with their messages to men! In this view of it, the meditative lyric at its best is but another name for the Christian idyl, such a collection as Mrs. Stowe's " Religious Poems " representing it in its normal function. In this view, indeed, Bryant and Longfellow and Emerson, in their high converse with truth and goodness as lyric poets, stand so closely next to the specifically religious

lyrists of our literature, to Heber and Mont-
gomery and Toplady, as to make the distinction
almost invalid, and include our best reflective
poems within the sacred circle of English hymnology.   How delicate the difference, after all,
as to their essential spirituality, between the
historic hymns of Hastings and Palmer and the
deeply religious verse of Lowell and Longfellow; between "The Rock of Ages" and "The
Vision of Sir Launfal," or "The Cathedral"!
Nor need this spiritual principle be expressed
in any one way or method, but, just because it
is spiritual, it is as varied and as free as the moral
nature of man.   In no sphere more than in this
does the personality of the poet reveal itself, it
lying within his own choice and the liberty of
his own literary instincts as to just how and how
fully he shall disclose this innermost quality of
himself and his work.   Chaucer expressed it in
one form, in the life-like sketches of " The Can-
terbury Tales "; Spenser, in another form, in his
great Protestant semi-epic; Milton, in still another; and Wordsworth, in still another.   John
Cowper wrote his "Task" and other secular
poems with as spiritual an intent as that with
which he wrote his hymns.   The same intensity

of moral earnestness and purpose characterizes
the most ordinary work of Mrs. Browning, while
the spiritual tone of Keats and Tennyson, though
just as really present, is uttered in a manner all
their own. So, in American verse, this difference
of manifestation is apparent, the meditative type
of Emerson being one thing and that of Bryant
another. So, do such poets as Lowell and Longfellow differ, as do Holmes and Whittier, Bayard
Taylor and Willis and Mrs. Stowe ; each of them,
however, in a true sense, recognizing the unworldly quality in verse and seeking to give it
some adequate embodiment. No attempts in
literature have been more unsuccessful than
those that have sometimes been made either to
ignore or to pervert this deep-seated instinct in
the nature of man, as the verse of Arnold and
Clough and Shelley and Wilde and Whitman
will attest. Sensuous verse or skeptical verse is
as untrue to the natural quality and aim of verse
as it is to the best natural instincts of man, and
only results in begetting in the souls of those
who subject themselves to it dissatisfaction with
themselves and the world.

A final word is in place to this effect: that
lyric verse, in its higher reflective and spiritual

forms, affords a study second to no other in all
that pertains to purity of soul and the quickening
of the inner and better life. Its special function
is to secure to the reader what Longinus has
called " elevation of thought and feeling," lifting
the whole being for the time outside of itself,
its trials and struggles and cares, into the upper
air of mental and moral peace. It is what a
modern writer has called " this interpenetration
of supernal radiance " that sets the soul free,
illumines all that is dark, eliminates all that is
low and belittling, and opens the way widely to
the clearer vision of God and truth. It is the
poetry of the affections, of the profoundest instincts of men, of human hope and aspiration,
of those " breathings from the depths " of which
De Quincey writes, and what he himself so pas-
sionately and vainly struggled to embody in
human language.

" Epic verse reaches at times sublimer heights
of mental outlook, and dramatic verse, on its
tragic side, assays a bolder and more impressive
function ; but it is reserved for the lyric, in a
quieter and more conservative manner, to find
its way into the most interior recesses of the
heart and minister to our most urgent spiritual

needs." To the clergy and the laity, to the special student of literature, and to every lover of good books, this spacious and inviting field is open. It will be an auspicious day indeed for the modern world when such an order of literature as this is appreciated at its full worth, and takes its rightful place in every home and library as superior to the lower and more transient literature of the time.

WILLIAM CULLEN BRYANT

William Cullen Bryant

1794-1878.

CHAPTER SECOND.

WILLIAM CULLEN BRYANT.

THE critics are still busy in determining which of all the historic and accepted divisions of verse may be said to be the greatest: whether it is the epic, as hitherto generally held; or the dramatic, as much of later literary criticism holds; or the lyric, which has never been more carefully and appreciatively studied than it is now, and has never so stoutly contested the claims of supremacy made by any other poetic form. Be this as it may, this much can safely be conceded, that, as lyric verse is the oldest of all the forms, so it is the simplest, tenderest, and most impressive; appealing, as it does, to the deepest affections and sympathies of the human heart, its joys and sorrows, its loves and hates, its passions and aspirations, its hopes and fears, so as to leave no part of the complex na-

ture of man unvisited by its appeals. The rich
variety of its orders or classes is sufficient to reveal the spacious scope that it covers, and its
wondrous adaptability to all the phases of earthly
experience. In ode and sonnet, in pastoral and
elegy, in song and idyl, in one species or another, it finds a fitting medium for its expression, and also finds a ready entrance into the
most guarded recesses of the spirit of man.
The epic may surpass it in majesty of movement
and a corresponding dignity and grandeur of
effect, and the dramatic may surpass it, on its
tragic side, in a sublime seriousness of manner,
or a bold and startling revelation of human sin
and struggle; but neither of them is comparable
to it in that sweet and gracious influence it ex-
erts over all human faculties and feelings, in that
subdued and softening impressiveness of which
the restless spirit of humanity is in such urgent
need. It is in this special province of lyric verse
that our American literature finds its most attractive and fruitful field, so that it would be
difficult to collect a richer anthology of the
idyllic order than that given us in any well-se-
lected Lyrica Americana, while it is from this
side of verse, most of all, that the compass and

excellence of our poetic product are to be judged.
Beginning as far back as the days of Freneau
and Rodman Drake, it unfolds itself in the
pages of Poe and Halleck and Bryant and
Willis, on through the rich succession of our
leading lyrists in the persons of Emerson and
Longfellow, Whittier and Lowell, and the modern school of Lanier and Aldrich and Carleton
and Stedman, which later bards, it may be said
without hesitation, have been singing in as
strong and as sweet a key as did their great
historic forerunners in the golden age of our
native verse. Especially in the line of the descriptive and delineative has this poetic work
been of pronounced excellence, whether as representing the world of physical phenomena, in all
its variety of light and shade, of valley, stream,
and mountain, or the vastly wider world of
mental and spiritual phenomena, in its endless
diversity of thought and character and life.

Of all the historic forms which such a deline-
ation of human experience has assumed in lyric
verse, none is more characteristically American
or more impressive in its effects than what we
have termed the meditative, known at times as
didactic or ethical verse, as seen in the poems

of Wordsworth or Cowper. Its conspicuous
quality is its reflective tone and temper, that
quiet and pensive order of verse which arises
from the poet's undisturbed communings on
God and man and human life and destiny, and
appeals directly and profoundly to the most
intense experience of the reader. It would not
be amiss to call it subjective or introspective
verse, dealing with conscience and the moral
nature of man ; and in this view of it, as specifically homiletic in its type, it comes with sin-
gular aptness and force to those engaged in the
study and diffusion of truth. We know of no
species of poetry more germane to devout and
thoughtful minds than this, surcharged, as it is,
with moral meaning, and evoking, as it is read,
all the deepest ethical impulses of the soul.
Passing over, not infrequently, from the region
of the merely meditative into the richer region
of the spiritual, it assumes the character of sacred and devotional song, and lies closely next
to the specifically inspired verse of Scripture.
Much of the hymnology of the Christian
church is but a higher form of it, while, in its most
unspiritual expressions, it appeals directly to the
soul's purest sensibilities.   How often might the

monotony of the sermon be relieved by an apt
quotation from the lyric lines of Longfellow or
Lowell! How often, indeed, might a biblical
teaching be enforced or a homiletic hint be fast-
ened by such a reference to the reflective English and American poets! Moreover, what a
gracious and chastening effect would an experi-
mental acquaintance with such poetry have on
the distinctly intellectual life of the preacher
and teacher of truth, as it exalts the spiritual
over the mental, the utterances of the heart
over the language of the schools, and, for the
time being, makes one forget that he is not so
much a sermonizer or a student as he is a man
among men, a lover of goodness and of beauty,
an interpreter of human experience to his fel-
low-men! Here and there, a line from so lov-
able and thoughtful a bard as Whittier would
so point a moral as to make its impression deep
and permanent.

With these thoughts in mind, we turn instinctively to Bryant, our earliest notable poet in the
province of the meditative, and, in some re-
spects, not surpassed by any later name. Whatever may be the classification of his poems on

which different critics, from various points of
view, insist, this reflective feature is discernible.
Wittingly or unwittingly, he never allows us to
forget it; while, if we look carefully between
the lines, we find him saying that this is, after
all, the dominant purpose of his verse and of all
true verse.   In what may be termed his Hebraic
poems, such as " Rizpah " and " The Song of
the Stars," this quality is controlling ; so, in his
North American poems, as in " The Indian
Girl's Lament."   Even in his national verse,
such as " Our Country's Call " and " The Death
of Lincoln," the tone is of this thoughtful order,
as, also, in his " Translations " from the various
European tongues there is the evident presence
of the meditative.   No theme can be so secular
that he will not, ere he closes, remind us that it
has a moral purport, and should be so presented
and received.   This is significantly shown in the
manner in which he develops subjects taken from
the external world of organic and inorganic nature, so that it is scarcely too much to say that
these physical topics are as full of the higher
teaching and spirit as those that are distinctively
reflective.

How clearly this is seen in " Thanatopsis,"

his first great poem—a poem in which the
earthly and the unearthly are so conjoined and
fused that no dividing line can be discerned!
Our love of nature is to express itself in "communion with her visible forms"; the voice to
which we are summoned to listen is "a still
voice," and the natural world is used throughout the poem but as a symbol by which the
great realities of the supernatural world are set
before us and impressed upon us.

From those poems of a general descriptive
character that have for their purpose the por-
trayal of natural life and scenery, and also in-
volve this meditative element, the discerning
reader can scarcely choose amiss. Thus, in
"Autumn Woods," he sings, after describing
the purely physical beauties of the trees:

> "Ah! 'twere a lot too blest
>   Forever in thy colored shades to stray;
> Amid the kisses of the soft southwest
>   To rove and dream for aye;
> And leave the vain low strife
>   That makes men mad—the tug for wealth and power,
> The passions and the cares that wither life,
>   And waste its little hour."

So in "A Forest Hymn," with its rare combination
of epic majesty and lyric tenderness, as he sings:

"Father, Thy hand
Hath reared these venerable columns, Thou
Didst weave this verdant roof. Thou didst look down
Upon the naked earth, and, forthwith, rose
All these fair ranks of trees. . . .
My heart is awed within me when I think
Of the great miracle that still goes on
In silence round me—the perpetual work
Of Thy creation, finished, yet renewed
Forever. . . .
Be it ours to meditate
In these calm shades, Thy milder majesty,
And to the beautiful order of Thy works
Learn to conform the order of our lives."

Bryant seemed to be especially happy and at home in the composition of these forest hymns, in that they brought him face to face with nature, stirred within him all the finer feelings of the heart, and enabled him to worship God directly, without the intervention of priest or ritual.   He thoroughly believed that "the groves were God's first temples."   So, in such nature-poems as "The Evening Wind," "The Snow-shower," "The Song of the Sower," "The Return of the Birds," and "June." We have sometimes thought that we look in vain in English and American lyrics for anything richer in the line of reflective song than that which we find in "June" as it opens:

" I gazed upon the glorious sky
 And the green mountains round,
And thought that when I came to lie
 At rest within the ground,
'Twere pleasant that in flowery June,
When brooks send up a cheerful tune,
 And groves a joyous sound,
The sexton's hand, my grave to make,
The rich, green mountain-turf should break.

'And what if cheerful shouts at noon
 Come, from the village sent,
Or song of maids, beneath the moon,
 With fairy laughter blent?
And what if, in the evening light,
Betrothèd lovers walk in sight
 Of my low monument?
I would the lovely scene around
Might know no sadder sight nor sound.

" I know that I no more should see
 The season's glorious show,
Nor would its brightness shine for me,
 Nor its wild music flow;
But if around my place of sleep
The friends I love should come to weep,
 They might not haste to go.
Soft airs, and song, and light, and bloom,
Should keep them lingering by my tomb."

All this is simply matchless as an expression
of idyllic tenderness, rich poetic melody, and
impressive ethical teaching, so that we wonder

whether Bryant can be any more meditative and
suggestive when he leaves the province of material nature for the distinctive province of
moral teaching, as seen in such poems as " The
Ages," " The Future Life," " An Evening Reverie," and " The Flood of Years." Thus, in
" The Crowded Street," after describing the
restless movement to and fro that one can daily
see in a thronged thoroughfare, he closes with
the lines:

> " Each where his tasks or pleasures call,
>   They pass and heed each other not.
>   There is who heeds, who holds them all,
>   In His large love and boundless thought.
>
> " These struggling tides of life, that seem
>   In wayward, aimless course to tend,
>   Are eddies of the mighty stream,
>   That rolls to its appointed end."

Whatever the topic, method, meter, or specific purpose, Bryant thus insists that poetry fails
of its greatest mission if, with all its literary correctness and spirit, it does not succeed in ennobling the moral nature of man. How eminently wholesome and tonic, therefore, is all this
verse, lifting the soul of the reader to the higher
levels, where the air is clearer and the outlook

wider; repressing every unhallowed thought
and desire; keeping him in line with all that is
best; and especially needed in these latter days,
when poets and prose writers alike deem it far
too often a sign of literary weakness to exalt the
spiritual in art, and much prefer to cross the line
over into the region of the animal and fleshly!
Bryant and Whitman! What a contrast here
we have between the realism of the soul and the
realism of the senses; between lyric piety and
lyric coarseness; between " Thanatopsis " and
" Leaves of Grass."

HENRY WADSWORTH LONGFELLOW.

Henry W. Longfellow

1807–1882.

CHAPTER THIRD.

HENRY WADSWORTH LONGFELLOW.

IF we were to judge from a poet's ancestry and general antecedents what the character of his poetry ought to be, we should certainly say as to Longfellow that it should be eminently thoughtful and instructive; good poetry, in every sense of the word; the spontaneous expression of a good man with but one governing purpose in his verse—the doing good in the world in which Providence had placed him. His sturdy Puritan and Pilgrim lineage guaranteed this; the old Yorkshire stock to which he belonged in the line of John Alden and Priscilla Mullens guaranteed it; the mental and moral dower he received through his father, Stephen, and his mother, Zilpah Wadsworth, guaranteed it; the beautiful environment of his early days in the old-fashioned and cultured city of Portland, the

" dear old town " of his childhood, guaranteed
it ; while it may be said that there seemed to
be in his experience that combination of nature
and grace, of human and divine approval, of inherited blessing and acquired blessing, that set
all the currents of his being from the first stead-
ily toward what was best, and made it impossible for him to be any other than he was—one
of the cleanest, sweetest characters and sons of
song that any literature possesses. That when
a mere lad in his teens such a poet as the devout Cowper interested him, and such a prose
writer as the gentle Irving was a formative influence in his life, we are not at all surprised to
learn ; nor surprised further to learn that, though
a free-hearted, genuine New England boy, fond
of boyish sports and full of boyish ambitions,
he was also fond of turning aside, not infrequently, from the playground to the library,
from frolicking to musing, and early caught an
inspiring vision of the great future that was
awaiting him.   It is thus that in his charming
reflective and retrospective poem, " My Lost
Youth," written in middle manhood, he recalls
those secret musings in which he indulged as a
child at school :

" I remember the gleams and glooms that dart
  Across the school-boy's **brain**;
The song and the silence in the heart,
That in part are prophecies, **and in part**
  Are longings wild and vain.
And the voice of that fitful song
  Sings on, and is never still;
  ' **A** boy's will is the wind's will,
And the thoughts of **youth** are long, long thoughts.' "

It was in these "long, long thoughts" that
he indulged, half in boyish reverie and half in
serious purpose, wondering even then at these
"prophecies" of youth, these "longings" of
his soul for a something far beyond, into the
gradual revelation and realization of which a
gracious destiny was yet to lead him. All this
was singularly characteristic in its essential
gravity of manner and outlook, and naturally
deepened in its impressiveness in his college
days at Bowdoin, when he and Hawthorne,
that introspective boy, walked together through
the streets of quaint old Brunswick and out into
the open country, talking of college life and
youthful aspirations, and wondering what the
larger life of the great world without was to
bring them, and what, perchance, they in turn
were to bring to it. " If this institution," says

Hawthorne, in his novel " Fanshawe," " did not offer all the advantages of elder and prouder seminaries, its deficiencies were compensated to its students by the inculcation of regular habits and of a deep and awful sense of religion, which seldom deserted them in life." It was this deep religious sense that lay at the basis of Long-fellow's nature and found a discreet expression in all the phases of his later work. In such a prose work as " Outre-Mer," light and descriptive as it is, we are not surprised to note such papers as " Pere La Chaise," " The Baptism of Fire," and " The Devotional Poetry of Spain "; as in his romance " Hyperion," he writes of " The Christ of Andernach," " Curfew Bells," " Shadows on the Wall," and " The Footprints of Angels." In the charming tale " Kavanagh " there is a rich vein of suggestive teaching running through it all, as when he says of morality, that " without religion it is only a kind of dead reckoning—an endeavor to find our place on a cloudy sea by measuring the distance we have run, but without any observation of the heavenly bodies."

It is, however, when this sober-minded author enters fairly on his great poetic career

that he may be said to find himself and find
his readers, as through the avenue of lyric and
descriptive verse he unbosoms his soul to us as
it meditates on God and man and human life
and destiny. There is a sense in which all his
lyric verse might fitly come under the title of
one of his earliest and most notable poems,
" A Psalm of Life," as it makes reality and
earnestness the great factors of character and
guiding principles of action. From his first collection of poems, " The Voices of the Night,"
in 1839, to his last collection, " In the Harbor,"
in 1882, the year of his death, this meditative
feature is always present, and, often, prominent,
and ever seen connected with a genial, cheerful,
hopeful view of life and duty and human history.
Not the faintest trace do we find here of the
morbid and morose, as in the school of Arnold
and Clough and Swinburne and Poe; nothing
of the pessimistic wail of the disappointed world-
ling, as in the school of Byron; no unhallowed
commingling of the sensual and the supersensual, as in the poetry of Shelley and Whitman;
and no merely pedantic attempt, in his most
serious utterances, to lose the poet in the
preacher, or, at all hazards, to point a moral,

after the manner of Martin Tupper, or that
of Pollock, in "The Course of Time." The
"Night Thoughts" of Edward Young may de-
serve the stinging sarcasm of Voltaire for their
enforced exhortations to duty, but not so "The
Voices of the Night" by Longfellow. Even
Bryant, in his best poetic work, failed, at times, in
this respect, where his more gifted contemporary
never failed, nor is there an author in American
letters, if, indeed, in British, who has written so
much and so ably within the sphere of purely
meditative verse, and so succeeded in keeping
wholly this side the line of the merely moralistic,
and within the safer and more attractive province
of poetry. All the more, however, has he succeeded in stamping upon our native verse a
meditative impress, from which it cannot and
would not divert itself in any later poetic era.
Whatever classification may be made of Longfellow's poems, as descriptive, dramatic, and
lyric, it is the lyric order that is the most common, most pronounced, most in keeping with the
poet's genius and taste, and most appreciated by
all those who have at heart the permanent suc-
cess of the author. Some of these lyrics take a
national form, as his tribute to " President Gar-

field"; some, the legendary form, as, "The Burial of the Minnesink"; some, the form of the ballad and sonnet, as the lines to Dante and Keats; while by far the most frequent and satisfactory expression of these idyllic verses is in the line of the meditative and moral. Here he was himself, thoroughly at home, and made his readers at once at home with him. We may thus turn over the leaves of his poetry almost at random to find fitting illustration of the fertility of his genius in the expression of human senti-ment. Thus, in that beautiful lyric, "Footsteps of Angels," beginning:

> " When the hours of day are numbered,
>   And the voices of the night
> Wake the better soul, that slumbered,
>   To a holy, calm delight ; "

and ending with equal tenderness:

> " Oh, though oft depressed and lonely,
>   All my fears are laid aside
> If I but remember only
>   Such as these have lived and died."

So, in such selections as " The Reaper and the Flowers," " God's-Acre," " The Rainy Day," " The Old Clock on the Stairs," " The Psalm of

Life," and "Resignation," with its familiar opening:

> " There is no flock, however watched and tended,
>   But one dead lamb is there;
> There is no fireside, howsoe'er defended,
>   But has one vacant chair."

Even in his translations this governing purpose is visible, as in " The Children of the Lord's Supper" and "The Good Shepherd." So, outside the province of the lyric proper, he is the same contemplative bard, musing over the great problems of the soul of man, as in " Evangeline " and " Hiawatha." In his dramatic trilogy " Christus," including " The Golden Legend," " The Divine Tragedy," and " New England Tragedies," this profound passion of his heart is everywhere apparent; so that, after all, the lyric governs the dramatic, and reveals the true direction of the poet's powers. His affectionate attitude toward children, and his lines written on their behalf, serve but to indicate still more fully this sensitive element in his nature and the " soul of goodness " that was in him, so that he is claimed by the young as by the old, evincing the fact that he succeeded in impressing all classes without passing to the extreme either of frivolity

or moroseness. It is not strange, indeed, that
the poet has somewhat suffered here at the hands
of the cynic and the ultra-critical, charged, as he
has been, with being moralistic and edifying to
a fault. It may be so, and yet who of us would
eliminate it from his verse, or modify in one iota
the primary purpose of his poetry! Moreover,
so sweet and gracious was his personality that
what in others would have been resented by the
reader as " church-steeple " exhortation is received at his hands with gratitude. With him,
as with Whittier, against whom the same accusa-
tion has been spoken, there was no sharp distinction between secular and sacred verse. All
verse was sacred, and the writing of it was accepted as a moral trust, so that " The Belfry at
Bruges," " Nuremburg," " The Building of the
Ship," and " Christmas Bells " were as instinct
with sacred purpose as were " The Two Angels " and " The Ladder of St. Augustine." To
think of Longfellow writing verse or prose as
Byron wrote it, or to write it for any other purpose than thereby to do good and cheer the lives
of good men, is quite out of the question, even
if in so doing he, at times, provoked adverse criticism, and, at times, sacrificed intellectual vigor to

the sway of human sentiment. As he says in
" Kavanagh," " In character, in manner, in style,
in all things, the supreme excellence is simpli-
city ; " and he adds, " Many people judge of the
power of a book by the shock it gives their feelings." How characteristically absent from the
verse before us is anything that would shock
the most delicate nature! How true it is to all
the best and deepest instincts of the soul; and
as the lines run on in their even, quiet way, what
hope and comfort they bring, what calm to
the troubled spirits, what encouragement to the
despondent, as the reader feels for the time that
he is communing with a friend rather than pe-
rusing the literary product of an author! Such
verse as this, we have said, is eminently adapted
to the clergy in their contemplative life and
spiritual work, and eminently adapted, we may
add, to what Mr. Bryce has called this " Age of
Discontent," this restless, overbusy, bustling, and
blustering age, looking on every hand for excit-
ing scenes and events, rating men and measures
according to the stir that they awaken, and protesting in emphatic words against the dull com-
monplace of modern civilization. What, we may
seriously inquire, is to become of us, if these

newsmongers and curiosity-seekers are to have
their way and set the form of modern life!
What, especially, is to issue in literature, and,
most of all, in verse, if this din of the market-
place is to prevail, and the value of poetry be
based on its efficacy in ministering to this insatia-
ble spirit of unrest! It was precisely against this
growing tendency that Emerson so courageously
spoke and wrote as he contended for the domi-
nance of "spiritual laws" in every sphere of
human effort. So did Longfellow live and write
"in the still air of delightful studies," and so does
the study of his verse soften and subdue our
peaceless spirits.

There is such a thing as restful reading, and
the poetry before us is a notable example, as is
all that verse which is prevailingly meditative.
Such an order of reading is more than restful.
It purifies as well as pacifies the mental and
moral nature, awakens within the soul all the
holier affections and impulses, brings it into sympathetic relation with all that is best in life and
song, and for a while, at least, uplifts us

> " Above the smoke and stir of this dim spot,
> Which men call Earth."

RALPH WALDO EMERSON.

R. Waldo Emerson

1803–1882.

CHAPTER FOURTH.

RALPH WALDO EMERSON.

RALPH WALDO EMERSON is thought of, perhaps, by the great majority of American readers
and literary students, as a writer whose work is
confined to the sphere of prose miscellany, the
author of profound papers on Plato and Shakespeare, and such abstract topics as ability, origin-
ality, and greatness. His most important work,
it is true, is in prose, though no reader can be
said to know Emerson fully who is not familiar
with that limited but characteristic contribution
that he has made to the volume of our native
verse, such a contribution being especially interesting in that his prose and verse were at length
so mutually interactive. In no particular was
this influence of the one upon the other more
marked than along those meditative lines that
we are now following. Critics have emphasized

correctly the contemplative type of Emerson's essays and of his prose style in general. The themes that he treats are sufficient evidence of this, as seen in " Spiritual Laws," " Character," " Inspiration," " Religion," " Worship," and " Immortality," while subjects the most secular and practical are approached and discussed in the same sobriety of spirit and with the same high intent. His clerical ancestry back through successive generations was a partial explanation of this. His study of theology, his ordination to the ministry, and his active experience in ministerial work, go far to explain it; while, quite apart from such antecedents and personal duties, he was constitutionally and profoundly meditative as a man and as an author, pre-inclined to the subjective and cogitative. His philosophy was introspective, his style and teaching were introspective, so that when he sat down to the composition of verse it would have been unnatural for him to have written anything other than reflective verse.

Critics have classified his poems as descriptive, national, and autobiographic. The fact is that, from first to last, they are meditative—simply the way in which the thoughtful Emerson

expressed his musings through the medium of
metrical language, whether the topic be in itself
reflective, as " The Problem " or " Destiny," or
whether in its character far removed from that,
as " My Garden " or " The Song of Nature."

The celebrated Greek critic, Longinus, sums
up all the essential elements of poetry and art
in the one word " sublimity," or, as he interprets
it etymologically, elevation of idea, feeling, and
expression. No one word could better set forth
the Emersonian spirit and purpose, insomuch
that all his mental and moral activities met and
were fused in this one generic principle. In the
best sense of the term, his poetry was dignified,
lifted high above all that was base and belittling,
and ever looking higher, if so be it might see the
face of God. It is in this sense that his philosophy has been called transcendental. His
poetry was such, even to the extent of being
Platonic, and, at times, mystic. No man or author was to him representative or worth the attention of the reader in whom this supernal quality was not more or less distinctive, as he saw
it in Goethe and Shakespeare and Plato. In
discussing what he calls " The Uses of ' Great
Men,' " he finds these " uses " beneficial to the

race just to the degree in which they raise the
eyes of men from earth to heaven, and induce
a reverent contemplation of the truth.   One of
the explanations of Emerson's occasional ob-
scurity both in prose and verse is found in the
fact that his thoughts were too elevated for
verbal embodiment, in accordance with Kant's
definition of sublimity, " the attempt to express
the infinite in the finite."   His conception of the
nature and office of poetry was of this supersensual, extramundane order.   Thus, in his "Fragments on the Poet and the Poetic Gift," he writes
to those who would attempt in verse to reach and
express the truth :

> " Shun passion, fold the hands of thrift,
>   Sit still, and Truth is near ;
>   Suddenly it will uplift
>   Your eyelids to the sphere ;
>   Wait a little ; you shall see
>   The portraiture of things to be."

It was this uplifting of the eye, in truly Miltonic
manner, to the vision of the sphere, to the partial
view, at least, of the infinities and immensities,
on which he zealously insisted as essential to the
first idea of a poet's function, applying peculiarly
to the poet what he writes of every true inquirer

" Around the man who seeks a noble end,
Not angels, but divinities, attend."

Herein is found one of the most potent reasons
for a knowledge of the poetry of Emerson on
the part of every high-minded man, and herein
one of its strongest claims upon the attention of
the clergy, in that the effect of it is spiritually
invigorating and exalting. No man can read
it intelligently and sympathetically and not be
made the purer and nobler thereby, and it is in
this spirit, primarily, that it is to be perused. If
we come to it as we come to the poetry of
Holmes or Lowell, or even as to that of the
gentle and gracious Whittier, we shall come
amiss. Even Bryant and Longfellow are meditative in a different way. No poet is more unique
than Emerson in the specific tone and quality of
his contemplative verse, as no other poet can for
a moment be mistaken for him. We should as
little look in any other American bard for such
poems as " The Sphinx," " The World," " Soul,"
" Sursum Corda," and " Brahma," as look in
Emerson for " Evangeline" or " Snow-bound."
On certain broad lines of poetic effort these various poets meet and commune, but as each of
them may be said to have a sphere of his own,

Emerson, of all others, occupies some territory absolutely alone, and will admit of no intruder, and this exclusive area is especially that in which poetic sublimity rises to its highest level. Hence, we come amiss to such a poetic seer if we come to be merely interested or entertained, or to find the conditions of what is known as readable and popular verse. Merely to be readable no poet ever aimed less directly than Emerson. Great ideas were latent within him, striving toward expression. Great ideals were before him, toward the realization of which he was ever aiming, but all without a thought of personal fame or of a large literary constituency or even the progress of letters, or of anything save the utterance of truth for the truth's sake and the highest good of man. A few citations from his verse will confirm these statements to every intelligent reader. Thus in " Good-By " he writes:

> " Good-by to Flattery's fawning face ;
>   To Grandeur, with his wise grimace ;
>   To upstart Wealth's averted eye ;
>   To supple Office, low and high ;
>   To crowded halls, to court and street ;
>   To frozen hearts and hasting feet ;
>   To those who go and those who come ;
>   Good-by, proud world! I'm going home.

Oh, when I am safe in my sylvan home,
I tread on the pride of Greece and Rome;
And when I am stretched beneath the pines,
Where the evening star so holy shines,
I laugh at the lore and pride of man,
At the sophist schools and the learned clan;
For what are they all, in their high conceit,
When man in the bush with God may meet."

There is in lines such as these an almost Mosaic or Hebraic element, scorning all contact with what is merely material and worldly, and making communion with God and the good the one central business of life. Wealth and station and the best that earth can offer are as nothing in comparison with love and adoration and worship and the daily contemplation of the divine. So, he writes in " Woodnotes ":

" Go where he will, the wise man is at home;
His hearth the earth, his hall the azure dome;
Where his clear spirit leads him, there's his road,
By God's own light illumined and foreshowed."

This reads as if from Bryant's " Thanatopsis," only possessing a deeper meaning and pulsating with a more vigorous spiritual life. How much like Bryant his love of solitude in the depths of the forests and the hills, as he sings:

> " Whoso walks in solitude
>   And inhabiteth the wood,
>   Choosing light, wave, rock, and bird
>   Before the money-loving herd,
>   Into that forester shall pass
>   From these companions, power and grace!"

It was the " money-loving herd " that he instinctively shunned, protesting that life could not be reduced to a commercial basis, and that it was worth living only to the degree in which one could rise above its lower levels to the vision and love of the best.   In his lines on " May-day," " The Adirondacks," " Nature," the theistic verges closely on the pantheistic, as he sees "the front of God" wherever he looks, and insists that, if we but listen closely, we can hear the voices of the spheres and stars:

> " Over his head were the maple buds,
>   And over the tree was the moon,
>   And over the moon were the starry studs
>   That drop from the angels' shoon."

As he sings in his " Fragments on the Poet":

> " Let me go where'er I will,
>   I hear a sky-born music still."

No couplet could better express the essential spirit of the personality and poetry of Emerson,

with his heart and ear ever open to catch the sound
of that " sky-born music " that he loved to hear.

> " It sounds from all things old,
>   It sounds from all things young,
> From all that's fair, from all that's foul,
>   Peals out a cheerful song.
> It is not only in the rose,
>   It is not only in the bird,
> Not only where the rainbow glows,
>   Nor in the song of woman heard.
> But in the darkest, meanest things
> There alway, alway, something sings."

This " something " was the voice of God in the
world, the clear and unmistakable note from
Heaven, calling men aside from sin and care and
worldly ambitions to the meditation and worship
of God.   No din of the market-place or crowded
street could be so loud as to prevent the hear-
ing of this clear call from above, and no science,
philosophy, literature, art, or life could be accepted that did not hear and heed this voice
from Heaven.   Emerson called himself a Christian theist.   His verse is thus Christianly theistic,
conceived and composed under the guidance of
those spiritual laws which he was so fond of
stating and impressing.   Evincing something
of Shelley's supernaturalism, he carefully keeps

this side the dangerous line which Shelley so often crosses, in the safer and saner company of Milton and Wordsworth and Bryant. If, indeed, he ever errs, his error is itself pardonable, in that we discern the overmastering purpose to exalt the divine above the human, and vitally connect poetry and all literature with the celestial verities. One of Matthew Arnold's most famous papers is on Emerson, in which he takes occasion, somewhat cynically, to depreciate his work and art. How vastly superior, however, is the American poet to the British in that profound spirituality of manner and purpose of which we are speaking, so that where the one keeps his eye clearly on the wisdom and beneficence of God, the other first doubts divine truth and then questions his own doubts, until poet and reader alike are lost in an endless maze of vagaries!

So have Carlyle and Emerson been brought into conspicuous relationship by that notable correspondence between them which is one of the treasures of modern literature, and yet, here again, how serene and uplifting the moral influence of the Concord poet as compared with that hesitating and skeptical attitude assumed by his British contemporary whenever he attempts to

deal with the fundamental problems of human
life! He warned young men against the appar-
ently successful principles of Napoleon, because
he was "the man of the world." He defends
Swedenborg as he does simply from his passionate love for the supernal in doctrine and life,
while, with all his admiration for Goethe, he
takes exception to him because "he has not as-
cended to the highest grounds from which genius has spoken, has not worshiped the highest
unity, and is incapable of a self-surrender to
the moral sentiment." In his pages on "The
Preacher" he laments that "the venerable and
beautiful traditions in which we were educated
are losing their hold on human belief," and
prophesies that "the next age will behold God
in the ethical laws."

Thus, in prose and verse alike, this New England apostle of truth, as he conceived, wrote and
strove for the larger and better things, and aimed
to lift the world somewhat above itself to the
thought of God and goodness and purity and love.

Emerson was more than a merely meditative
poet. . He was the real poet-preacher of his time,
"approbated," as he would say, to the ministry
of right and truth.

EDGAR ALLAN POE.

Edgar A Poe

1809–1849.

CHAPTER FIFTH.

EDGAR ALLAN POE.

As the recently issued " Letters of Matthew Arnold" serve to call renewed attention to his interesting life and work, so the latest and best edition of Poe's works, by Stedman & Woodbery, invites us once again to examine the personality and literary product of this fascinating author. Rarely does a name come before the student of literature that elicits so much sympathy and earnest inquiry, if so be something like justice may be done him as a man and writer.

Though, as Whipple states it, " he was cursed by an incurable perversity of character," the more we reflect and investigate, the more inclined we are to attribute most of his errors to this inherited curse, and, less and less, to malicious purpose and preference. His nature was complex and contradictory—a kind of battle-

73

ground for discordant elements. So imperious,
at times, that he could say, " My whole nature
utterly revolts at the idea that there is any being in the universe superior to myself," he would,
at the next moment, evince a docility of spirit
and control of temper as attractive as it was surprising. At times disingenuous, and brooking
no appeal from his decisions, he would, again,
be as tender as a woman in his considerate regard for others. Hence, the different estimates
of which he has been the subject, and, hence, the
safety of the prophecy that, while critics judge
and readers read, Edgar Allan Poe's character
and writings will be, as Arnold would say, " interesting." The constant demand, as the pub-
lishers tell us, for his prose and verse compels
the conviction that there is that in what he was
and what he wrote that appeals both to educated
and popular taste, and holds him safely in his
place as one of the few prominent names in
American letters.

Our present purpose has to do exclusively
with Poe as a poet, no special reference being
made either to his work as a writer of tales or
as a literary critic.

We are dealing, moreover, with lyric verse

only, and, within the lyric province itself, only with that specific type that is meditative. Poe's poetic product is by no means extensive. As far as mere number of poems is concerned, they are not more than half a hundred titles, while the most of these are below the average length. As far as poetic class or form is concerned, they are practically confined to the kind we are discussing,—the lyric,—no epic being included, and, with the exception of the unpublished poem, " Scenes from Politian," no dramatic verse, though in " The Raven" there is a marked dramatic cast and effect. As a poet, moreover, his fame may be said to rest upon a very few productions, written in the closing decade of his brief life of forty years, these conspicuous examples being such, not simply because of what they are in themselves, but also of that poetic " promise and potency " that they are seen to contain. He was possessed of the genuine poetic sense, " the sense of beauty," the sense of form, of ideal, of esthetic art.

Early in life he wrote: " I am a poet, if deep worship of all beauty can make me one. I would give the world to embody one half the ideas afloat in my imagination." He went so

far, indeed, as to exalt beauty above truth, as the
end of the poet's function, poetry having been
with him, as he says, " not a purpose, but a passion." His very definition of poetry as " the
rhythmical expression of beauty " includes this
principle as dominant.

We are dealing with American lyrics of the
meditative order, and it is scarcely too much to
say that, as Poe's poems are mainly lyrics, his
lyrics are mainly meditative, of that pensive and
radically ethical type rightly expected of a man
who spent his life in aiming to solve the problems
and perplexities of his being. Never did a man
start and prosecute these problems more pas-
sionately and persistently than Poe, and often
awakening our deepest sympathy and pity, as he
stands face to face with these problems, utterly
unable to solve them. In prose or verse, and
even in criticism, Poe was, out and out, a psychol-
ogist, a student and an interpreter of character,
peering deeper and deeper into the secret recesses of the human heart. What writer has so
dissected motive and conduct as Poe has done
in his mystic and yet realistic tales, as in " Bere-
nice," " The Imp of the Perverse," and " Tell-
tale Heart," and other sketches! What a stu-

dent he is of causes and effects, of the relation
of environment to character, of good and evil
tendencies, of heredity and destiny—in a word,
of man and of men!

So when we speak of his verse as reflective,
we simply call attention to the fact that he is as
a poet what he is as a prose writer and a man—
a close and a discriminating observer of human
personality and history, a diagnostician in the
realm of mind. As a recent critic has expressed
it, "his poetry is a cry from the land of Poe."
It is, indeed, a "cry," taking, sometimes, the
strong, demonstrative form of unrepressed emotion over lost opportunities and unrealized
ideals, and, at times, heard as a deep, suppressed
sobbing, as if his heart would break over his own
hapless state and that of those he loved as he
loved his own life. It is this "cry" that, as we
read, we hear and must hear, and which so often
rebukes all criticism, and summons us, despite
ourselves, to the poet's defense and positive
praise. It is this power of sympathy that has
turned the heads of the wisest among us, as
they assert that, "of all American writers, Poe
has made the deepest, and, in all probability, the
most lasting impression upon the world's imagi-

nation;" "that he is the solitary fixed star in
our firmament," "the most distinct of American
geniuses."

With this meditative element in view, it is interesting to turn to the poems of Poe, to note its
presence and impressiveness. The very titles
of many of the poems reveal it, such as "A
Dream," "Spirits of the Dead," "Alone," "The
Haunted Palace," "To One in Paradise," "The
Valley of Unrest," "The Sleeper," "Silence,"
"A Dream within a Dream," and others; while
poems such as "The Bells" and "Ulalume" and
"Eulalie" and "The Raven" give no indication
in their titles of the wealth of thoughtfulness
that is in them.

How touching his early poem, "Alone"!

> " From childhood's hour I have not been
>   As others were; I have not seen
>   As others saw; I could not bring
>   My passions from a common spring;
>   From the same source I have not taken
>   My sorrow; I could not waken
>   My heart to joy at the same tone;
>   And all I loved, I loved alone.
>   Then, in my childhood, in the dawn
>   Of a most stormy life, was drawn
>   From every depth of good and ill
>   The mystery which binds me still."

So, his early poem, " A Dream," written in the
same minor and reminiscent strain :

> " In visions of the dark night
>   I have dreamed of joy departed ;
> But a waking dream of life and light
> Hath left me broken-hearted.

> " That holy dream, that holy dream,
>   While all the world were chiding,
> Hath cheered me as a lovely beam
> A lonely spirit guiding."

His poems entitled " Dreamland " and " A
Dream within a Dream " strike the same contemplative and semidespondent note, as if crav-
ing human sympathy in his loss of courage and
hope in the struggle of life. So, in " Lenore "
and " Silence " and " Ulalume " and " The
Haunted Palace," a similar sentiment prevails.

One of the most suggestive lyrics which Poe
has written of this pensive type is that entitled
" A Hymn," addressed as it is to the Virgin
Mary :

> " At morn, at noon, at twilight dim,
> Maria, thou hast heard my hymn!
> In joy and woe, in good and ill,
> Mother of God, be with me still!
> When the hours flew brightly by,
> And not a cloud obscured the sky,

My soul, lest it should truant be,
Thy grace did guide to thine and thee.
Now, when storms of Fate o'ercast
Darkly my Present and my Past,
Let my Future radiant shine
With sweet hopes of thee and thine."

Even his beautifully rhythmic poem "The Bells" has in it, with all its "merriment," this essential element of pathos, and

"What a tale of terror, now, their turbulency tells!
What a world of solemn thought their monody compels!"

How touching the tribute that he gives, in his poem "To My Mother," to her who, as the mother of Virginia, had been to him more than his own mother, and done for him what no other one could have done!

One of his most significant meditative lyrics is that on "The Colosseum," reminding us in some of its lines of Byron's reflections on the same inspiring theme:

"Type of the antique Rome!   Rich reliquary
Of lofty contemplation left to Time
By buried centuries of pomp and power!
At length—at length—after so many days
Of weary pilgrimage and burning thirst
(Thirst for the springs of love that in thee lie),

I kneel, an altered and an humble man,
Amid thy shadows, and so drink within
My very soul thy grandeur, gloom, and glory!"

As to "The Raven," his greatest poem and lyric, the reader need not be told that it is surcharged with subdued and passionate interest, a "cry" out of the depth of his soul for his "lost Lenore," the "cry" deepening in pathetic tenderness as

"The silence was unbroken, and the stillness gave no token."

Thus the poetry runs on in this suppressed and affecting key, eliciting, as we read it, our heart-felt pity for one who seemed forever to utter unheeded cries for light and help, and plunging from darkness, and deeper darkness, as his pitiful life developed. It is this fact more than any other that explains the statement of a living critic: "What Poe actually accomplished in poetry has been unsatisfactory to the academic mind; to human nature it has been immensely and persistently fascinating." It is this that explains the apparent anomaly that, debauchee that he was, "his teaching was neither the disgusting sensualism of Byron nor the refined licentiousness of Shelley; it was a plea for beauty pure and simple." "He was never low enough to praise the accuracy with which a poet, a painter, or a novelist bombarded the sanctity of marriage, or to excuse the subtlety with which a so-called realist poisoned, in the name of truth, the deepest fountains of character." All this is true, and forces us in the name of Christian charity to put the best construction on his character, and in the last analysis to judge his verse somewhat independently of his life.

Be this as it may, however, what profoundly interests us as we read is this meditative attitude of Poe, as, "deep into the darkness peering," he seeks to know something of the divine and the human; of life and immortality and duty and destiny, consulting every oracle and interpreting every sign, if so be he may rise at once and forever from what he calls "the Valley of Unrest" to the upper land of clearer outlook and firmer footing. In this respect, he is the Arthur Hugh Clough of American verse, the seeker for certainty through doubt and fear, deeming it to be his appointed lot

> "To spend uncounted years of pain,
> Again, again, and yet again,

In working out in heart and brain
The problem of our being here."

A word, in closing, to this effect should be
said : that, of all the meditative American lyrists
whose verse we are examining, Poe is the only
one whose poetry has in it anything of the
abnormal and unhealthful, and must, therefore,
be read with the facts full in view. It is not
enough to say of him what we have said in the
line of exculpation and defense ; nor to say that,
" however lewd the man may have been, there
is no pandering to lewdness in his writings ;
that, physiologically a degenerate, his degeneracy
never reached his understanding of the function
of art." These distinctions, if indeed valid, are
too close for comfort and moral safety, and we
need and demand as our highest models poets
and men who compel us less frequently to assume the defensive and offer repeated apology.

Poe and Bryant, Poe and Emerson, Poe and
Longfellow, Poe and Whittier—what contrasts
are here, and all within the region of reflective
verse! How radically different their ethical
points of view, and with how different a spirit
do they face and aim to solve the pressing questions of life! Meditative the verse is, and preg-

nant with moral teaching, but with what different feelings do we rise from the reading of the
respective moralists!

> " And the fever called ' living '
>   Is conquered at last."

writes the disconsolate Poe in his beautiful lyric
"For Annie." We must look in vain in the
poetry of any other representative American
poet for so hopeless a sentiment as that.

JOHN GREENLEAF WHITTIER.

John G. Whittier

1807-1892.

CHAPTER SIXTH.

JOHN GREENLEAF WHITTIER.

OF all the poets of America, no one would be more promptly and naturally selected as, by way of distinction, a contemplative author, than Whittier, the Quaker poet, the "prophet bard," the "Hebrew poet of the nineteenth century." His first published poem, "Sicilian Vespers," is strikingly suggestive of that quiet, pensive habit of mind which characterized him in earlier and later life, and made it impossible for him to be any other than serenely meditative on the great questions of life and destiny that appealed to his reverent mind. In Longfellow's beautiful tribute to Whittier on his seventieth birthday, in the poem entitled "The Three Silences of Molinos," this dominant feature is worthily portrayed:

"Three Silences there are: the first of speech,
The second of desire, the third of thought;

These Silences, commingling each with each,
Made up the perfect Silence that he sought
And prayed for, and wherein at times he caught
Mysterious sounds from realms beyond our reach.
O thou, whose daily life anticipates
The life to come, and in whose thought and word
The spiritual world preponderates,
Hermit of Amesbury! thou too hast heard
Voices and melodies from beyond the gates,
And speakest only when thy soul is stirred."

Whittier is, indeed, the " hermit-thrush" of our American song, and is never so much himself and so much to others as when embodying in verse these " melodies from beyond the gates."

From his honorable ancestry, the Greenleafs and Husseys and Batchelders, he had come by right to this inheritance of a clear eye for the inner light and an open ear to every hallowed voice, so that when he wrote in prose or verse, on secular or sacred themes, he always wrote as a disciple and lover of the truth, as an author with a message from God to men, and in the meditative manner of one of the Hebrew prophets.

It is indeed difficult for us to understand how his pacific and quiet spirit could bring itself, as it did, voluntarily into contact with the coarse political conflicts of the time, save as we remember that it was only thus that he could effect the beneficent work on behalf of national honor and the rights of man which it was given him to do. Indeed, it is questionable whether a reformer of sterner mold and more defiant methods would have so well succeeded when error was to be met by the simple force of truth, and human wrong to be righted by patience and love and conciliatory measures. It was thus that Whittier often succeeded where such aggressive spirits as Garrison failed, and in the heat and thick of the wildest passions of the populace preserved the peace of his spirit, the even tenor of his way, his faith in God and faith in man, and often by a simple national lyric secured results which balls and bayonets could not effect.

It was by these songs of " religious and artistic repose," as Kennedy terms them, that he won his way into the hearts of his very enemies, and endeared himself to the thousands whose cause he had espoused.

The verse of Whittier is, in a valid sense, lyric or idyllic from first to last, and to this degree has in it a distinctive reflective element, dealing with the hopes and fears, the joys and sorrows, the struggles and triumphs of men, and always with his eye upon that spiritual principle underneath them all and that spiritual outcome to which they all were working.

More specifically, his poems might be classified as national, lyric, and religious or ethical, including, respectively, such examples as " The Virginia Slave Mother," " Among the Hills," and " My Soul and I." No careful reader of Whittier, however, need be told that these distinctions are purely conventional, and that it is a distinction without a difference to tell us that " The Centennial Hymn " is national only, and " The Tent on the Beach " lyric only, while " Telling the Bees " is ethical and contemplative.

Among his poems called national are such titles as " Laus Deo," " The Reformer," " The Moral Warfare," and " The Exiles "; while such descriptive lyrics as " The River Path," " The Changeling," " St. Gregory's Guest," and " Among the Hills," are replete with sober reflection, and cannot be appreciatively read save by him who takes them up with clearness of spirit, and for high and noble ends. Among his poems, however, that have a pronounced meditative type, often assuming a specific religious impressiveness, may be cited "Questions of Life," "The Shadow and the Light," "Truth," "Revelation," "The Cry of a Lost Soul," "The Eternal Goodness," "At Last," "The Common Question," "The Crucifixion," "Trinitas," "Thy Will be Done," "Forgiveness," "Andrew Rykman's Prayer," and such Hebraic verses as "Ezekiel." These are poems surcharged with moral and spiritual life, and would scarcely be out of place under the category of American hymnology. In such a list as this it is almost invidious to make selections. A few representative lines may be cited.

Thus we read in the poem, "Trust":

> "The same old baffling questions! O my friend,
> I cannot answer them. . . .
> I have no answer for myself or thee,
> Save that I learned beside my mother's knee:
> All is of God that is, and is to be;
> And God is good. Let this suffice us still,
> Resting in childlike trust upon His will
> Who moves to His great ends unthwarted by the ill."

So, in the "Shadow and the Light":

> "Oh, why and whither? God knows all;
>   I only know that He is good,
> And that whatever may befall,
>   Or here or there, must be the best that could,

And dare to hope that he will make
 The rugged smooth, the doubtful plain;
His mercy never quite forsake,
 His healing visit every realm of pain;
Ah me! we doubt the shining skies,
 Seen through our shadows of offense,
And drown with our poor, childlike cries
 The cradle-hymn of kindly Providence."

So, in "Andrew Rykman's Prayer," one of the
most tender and holy utterances of Whittier's,
beginning:

 " Pardon, Lord, the lips that dare
  Shape in words a mortal's prayer!
  Father!   I may come to Thee
  Even with the beggar's plea,
  As the poorest of Thy poor,
  With my needs and nothing more;
  Yet, O Lord, through all a sense
  Of Thy tender providence
  Stays my failing heart in Thee
  And confirms the feeble knee.
  Hours there be of inmost calm,
  Broken but by grateful psalm,
  When I love Thee more than fear Thee,
  And Thy blessed Christ seems near me,
  With forgiving look, as when
  He beheld the Magdalen.
  Well I know that all things move
  To the spheral rhythm of love,
  That to Thee, O Lord of all!
  Nothing can of chance befall; "

and so on through lines of exquisite spiritual richness, so pertinently closing with the query:

> " Thus did Andrew Rykman pray.
>   Are we wiser, better grown,
>   That we may not, in our day,
>   Make his prayer our own? "

In his matchless lyric, " The Eternal Goodness," where shall we begin or end!

> " No offering of my own I have,
>   Nor works my faith to prove;
>   I can but give the gifts He gave,
>   And plead His love for love.
>   And so beside the Silent Sea
>   I wait the muffled oar;
>   No harm from Him can come to me
>   On ocean or on shore,
>   I know not where His islands lift
>   Their fronded palms in air;
>   I only know I cannot drift
>   Beyond His love and care. "

This is not only as choice lyric verse as can be found within the limits of English literature, but it is suffused and saturated with spiritual life, sanctified throughout by the presence of a holy trust in God and goodness, and an ever-present and a controlling desire to be of moral service to men. In no British or American verse has the border-line between the secular and the sacred been so narrow, nor has any poet been less subject than Whittier to the charge of carrying the secular to the extreme of the coarse and the frivolous, or the sacred to the extreme of the somber and morose. Poetry was with him nothing less than a divinely assigned vocation for the realization of the highest human ends. No prophet or preacher ever plied his calling with a more devoted consecration to the interests of truth and righteousness; so that, whatever his theme might be, he approached it and presented it in a reverent spirit, never allowing himself to descend to those shifts and devices by which so many authors seek to gain the popular ear. In his "Songs of Labor and Reform," as they are called, and in his "Anti-slavery Poems" and "Poems of Nature," as well as in his specifically subjective and ethical verse, there is found this same reflective and reverent vein running through them all, and thus giving them a character and adorning that definitely marked them from all the inferior forms of contemporary poetry.

He wrote on "Seed-time and Harvest," "The Fishermen" and "Lumbermen" and "Ship-

builders," " The River Path " and " Hazel Blos-
soms," " The Slave-ship," and " The Crisis,"
with his characteristic serenity and moral gravity, so as to carry the truth he was uttering
with impressiveness and effectiveness to the
hearts and consciences of men. Never has a
poet more thoroughly deserved to be called " the
poet of conscience," as he appealed directly and
continuously to the moral faculty, and to the
sense of right in man, to the convictions of justice and law and national obligation. It was
this feature more than all else that redeemed the
" Antislavery Poems " of Whittier from the criticism of being sentimental or indignant tirades
against an existing evil ; the fanatical outbursts
of a would-be reformer, whose better judgment
for the time was under the control of his passions
and prejudices. Never did a man hold himself
better in hand, or better know precisely what
he was doing and why he was doing it, than did
Whittier when penning such fiery invectives as
" The Hunters of Men," " Stanzas for the Times,"
" The Branded Hand," and " Clerical Oppres-
sors." It was, indeed, a holy war that he was
waging in those days and those verses, when
smooth-flowing lyrics on love and friendship

gave way by right to impassioned protests in the name of God against injustice and cruelty and violations of moral law.

> " Shall tongues be mute when deeds are wrought
>   Which well might shame extremest hell?
> Shall freemen lock the indignant thought?
>   Shall Pity's bosom cease to swell?
> Shall Honor bleed? shall Truth succumb?
> Shall pen and press and soul be dumb? "

So, in " The Crisis," he writes in similar strain

> " By all for which the martyrs bore the agony and shame,
> By all the warning words of truth for which the prophets came,
> By the Future which awaits us, by all the hopes which cast
>   Their faint and trembling beams across the blackness of the
>   Past,
> And by the blessed thought of Him who for earth's freedom
>   died —
>   O my people! O my brothers! let us choose the righteous
>   side."

This is Whittier, speaking, as Longfellow tells us, when his "soul is stirred," when his conscience is quickened, if so be he may quicken the conscience of others, and, to some degree, at least, rectify the wrongs that pass unrebuked before his eyes. We call this meditative verse, and so it is, not in the sense that it is subdued and subjective, as his lines on " Trust " and " The

Prayer-seeker " and " The Friends Burial," but
that it is the intense utterance of his reflections
on national history, as developing before him. As
he mused, the fire burned, and must reveal itself,
as it did, in the language of spiritual passion. In
this and kindred verse Whittier was not only a
political reformer, but a Christian reformer, and
sought what he sought in the name and for the
glory of God.

Attention has often been called to the domes-
ticity of Whittier's verse, the homeness of it, so
that, as we read it, we think of Burns in his
" Cotter's Saturday Night," or Allan Ramsay's
" Gentle Shepherd," and can, indeed, gather
from his pages a full-sized picture of the local
life of the New England of his day. They have
this reminiscent or retrospective element in
them, recalling the old days and the old friends
and the old scenes. In no form of his poetry
does this attractive meditative feature appear
more fully, taking on richer type and meaning
as the years go by and increasing age does its
mellowing and gracious work. Never outside
the limits of his native land, and but seldom beyond the borders of his own New England, he
was a son of the soil and a poet of the soil as but

few have been, so that all he spoke and wrote was English and New English to the core, and ever marked by the distinctive lineaments of its Puritan origin and home. He thus writes of "Maud Muller," "The Old Burying-ground," "In School-days," and "June on the Merrimac," with all the gusto of a New England boy; and would have us know in "Snow-bound" that, as the rigor of winter increased, the inside delights of the fireside were heightened, and he and his friends were happy all the livelong day and all the livelong year; nor amid all the joy does he allow us for a moment to forget it is to a kindly Providence over us that we owe all our earthly blessings, and must render daily praise and service.

In fine, so pronounced is this contemplative feature and so persistent is the poet in reminding his readers of their obligations to God and man, that the charge of extreme religiousness has been made against him, a charge that cannot be substantiated by the honest reader, but one, we are free to say, that Whittier would willingly have incurred rather than to have invited the criticism at the other extreme of a manifest want of moral motive.

In noting the meditative character of Whittier's verse, special reference should be made to what may be called his hymns. One of these is found in the poem entitled " The Wish of To-day," and opens with the lines:

> " I ask not now for gold to gild
>   With mocking shine a weary frame;
> The yearning of the mind is stilled;
> I ask not now for fame."

His " Eternal Goodness," from which we have already quoted, is substantially a hymn. The poem " Our Master " is virtually a hymn, and so embodied by Duffield in his " English Hymns":

> " Immortal Love, forever full,
>   Forever flowing free,
> Forever shared, forever whole,
>   A never-ebbing sea."

So, such poems as " The Star of Bethlehem," " Invocation," " Vesta," and " At Last," are easily classified under hymnology, both as to context and spirit, so illustrative are they of the mingling of praise and prayer, and, as Duffield states it, "come naturally, like the verses of Keble, into the service of the church."

What earlier or later poet, we may ask, has

wrought more effectively and lovingly in the
service of the church? His life from first to last
was ministerial, a worship and a ministry in one,
intense in its devotion to every good cause, and
actively instrumental in every line of Christian
effort.

Not a few worthy authors are now busily at
work in the expanding field of American letters,
men of genius in their way, and giving promise
of large and beneficent result; but where shall
we look to find a true successor of this old master of song, who sang as naturally as the birds
sing, and only for the divine glory and the common good!

JAMES RUSSELL LOWELL.

J. R. Lowell

1819-1891.

JAMES RUSSELL LOWELL.

MR. LOWELL, in so far as his poetry is concerned, is remembered, more especially, perhaps, by his " Biglow Papers" and " The Fable for Critics," the satirical and serio-comic character of each of these poems making them attractive to all classes of people. In neither of them, however, is there any distinctive presence of the contemplative element, so that readers of these productions only might be unwittingly led to assume that this was Lowell's only form of verse. A closer inspection of his poetry reveals the fact that the humorous and satirical are but a portion of his poetic product, the general descriptive and lyric feature being also prominent. Critics speak also of his national and legendary verse, in each of which classes, if regarded as distinct, as conspicuously in the lyric, the meditative tone and quality are, in fact, the most characteristic.

107

When Lowell is called " our new Theocritus," reference is made to the prominent presence of this idyllic quality. In his " Poems of Nature," so-called, as in his sonnets, his poems of sentiment and of religion, it is needless to note that the reflective phase is necessarily pronounced. Moreover, Mr. Lowell is reflective in his own way, and in fullest accord with his unique individuality as an author, even as Bryant and Emerson and Longfellow and Whittier and Holmes are, respectively, meditative. A contemplative sonnet from Lowell, such as the one beginning:

" Great truths are portions of the soul of man,"

or the one:

" There never yet was flower fair in vain,"

has in its lines and between the lines the peculiar Lowellian cast and character, meaning from Lowell something different from that which a similar sonnet would mean from any of his great contemporaries whom we are studying. We look in vain in Lowell for such subjective poems as Bryant's " Thanatopsis " and " The Flood of Years," or Emerson's " Sphinx " and " Brahma," or Longfellow's " Divine Tragedy," or Whittier's

"Toussaint l'Overture," or Holmes's "Living Temple." Each of these authors looks at the world and human life from his own point of view; has his own method of solving the pressing moral problems that confront him; insists upon the choice and use of his own phraseology; and is, in fact, as careful not to be confounded in his meditative verse with any other poet as he is not to be confounded with any other in any important sphere of authorship. Of the six poets mentioned, Lowell and Holmes are less contemplative than the others, both in their personality and poetry, and Holmes the least so of all. There is a spiritual fineness in Emerson not found in any of them, as there is a sweetness of temper in Whittier nowhere else discernible. If we may so express it, the meditative type of Holmes is that of a thoughtful man of the world, as compared with the more introspective type of such a poet as Longfellow, while Lowell may fitly be called the scholarly observer of the morals and manners of men. His reflections are from the standpoint of educated sense and taste, and always presented in attractive form. He is, by way of excellence, the cultured thinker, never forgetting in his musings and moralizings that he is a man of letters, at his study windows and among his books. It is this studied and artistic element that differentiates his meditative verse from that of others, and somewhat detracts from its value in the eye of readers whose natures are deeply emotional and quickly responsive to every impassioned appeal. For this reason, if for no other, Lowell's reflective poems will never have so vital a hold upon the hearts of men as those of Longfellow and Whittier.

In noting more particularly what Lowell has written of this subjective or pensive order, we find numerous examples of it in three out of the four volumes of his recently collected works—in "The Earlier Poems," in "Under the Willows," and in "Heartsease and Rue."

In the first of these collections are such poems as "Irene," "The Forlorn," "A Parable," his various sonnets, "A Legend of Brittany," "The Sower," "Extreme Unction," "Longing," and "The Vision of Sir Launfal." Thus, in "Irene," we read:

"Hers is a spirit deep, and crystal clear;
　　Calmly beneath her earnest face it lies,
　Free without boldness, meek without a fear,
　　Quicker to look than speak its sympathies.

Far down into her large and patient eyes
　I gaze, deep drinking of the infinite,
　　As, in the mid-watch of a clear, still night,
　I look into the fathomless blue skies."

So, in the lines in " Longing," he speaks a helpful word as he sings:

" Ah! let us hope that to our praise
　　Good God not only reckons
　The moments when we trust His ways,
　　But when the spirit beckons;
　That some slight good is also wrought
　　Beyond self satisfaction,
　When we are simply good in thought,
　　Howe'er we fail in action."

In the second collection are such examples
as " Godminster Chimes," " The Parting of the
Ways," " The Darkened Mind," " In the Twilight," and " The Foot-path." From the first
of these we read:

" Through aisles of long-drawn centuries
　　My spirit walks in thought,
　And to that symbol lifts its eyes
　　Which God's own pity wrought;
　From Calvary shines the altar's gleam,
　　The Church's East is there,
　The Ages one great minster seem,
　　That throbs with praise and prayer.

" And, as the mystic aisles I pace,
　　By aureoled workmen built,

> Lives ending at the Cross I trace
> Alike through grace and guilt;
> One Mary bathes the blessed feet
> With ointment from her eyes,
> With spikenard one, and both are sweet,
> For both are sacrifice."

In the third collection we emphasize his poems of affectionate tribute to Agassiz, Holmes, and Whittier, his " Das Ewig-Weibliche," " The Recall," " Absence," and " A Christmas Carol," written for Sabbath-school children, and full of suggestive biblical reference.

> " ' What means this glory round our feet,'
> The Magi mused, ' more bright than morn?'
> And voices chanted clear and sweet,
> ' To-day the Prince of Peace is born.'

> " ' What means that star?' the shepherds said,
> ' That brightens through the rocky glen?'
> And angels, answering overhead,
> Sang, ' Peace on earth, good-will to men.'

> " 'Tis eighteen hundred years and more
> Since those sweet oracles were dumb.
> We wait for Him, like them of yore;
> Alas! He seems so slow to come!

> " But it was said, in words of gold,
> No time or sorrow e'er shall dim,
> That little children might be bold
> In perfect trust to come to Him.

" All round about our feet shall shine
    A light like that the wise men saw
If we our loving wills incline
    To that sweet Life, which is the Law.

" So shall we learn to understand
    The simple faith of shepherds then,
And, clasping kindly hand in hand,
    Sing, ' Peace on earth, good-will to men.'

" And they who do their souls no wrong,
    But keep at eve the faith of morn,
Shall daily hear the angel sing,
    ' To-day the Prince of Peace is born.' "

From the publication of Milton's " Ode on the
Morning of Christ's Nativity," in 1629, to Whittier's " Christmas Carmen," we have no Christ
carol more beautiful than this, while it possesses
peculiar interest as coming from Lowell in the
way of a loving service to children. From
Longfellow we are led to look for such remem-
brances of childhood as he gives us in " The
Children's Hour " and other selections, of which
Whittier so sweetly sings in his " The Poet and
the Children," as Whittier himself, in his " Child
Songs " and elsewhere, is thoroughly at home
when writing for the young. In Lowell, however, such a strain is less frequently heard and
less in accord with his distinctive mental and

literary type, and this, when it is found, as in this exquisite poem, is all the more impressive. His poetry fittingly closes in meditative manner with the quotation on his " Sixty-eighth Birthday " :

> " As life runs on, the road grows strange
>   With faces new, and near the end
>   The milestones into headstones change;
>   'Neath every one we find a friend."

Those most intimate with Lowell could not but mark, as his life drew on toward its close, how some of the less attractive features of his earlier years were modified; how scholastic reserve gave place by gradual process to a more genial bearing, and the mellowing influences of years came at length to do their perfect work.

In speaking of the reflective quality of Lowell's verse, as of that of his noted American contemporaries, it occurs to us to say that this contemplative spirit is thoroughly germane to the mission of the poet in the world of letters as a specifically spiritual mission. When it is remembered that the earlier forms of verse were religious, that the minstrel was often the prophet and the priest, that the poet as such was supposed to be in communion with the invisible world, that the ideal is essential to the very conception of

poetry, it is not strange if we should find in all
standard verse, epic, dramatic, and lyric, the supernal, spiritual feature expressing itself in meditative forms, and, most especially, in the lyric.
It would seem to require a special effort on the
poet's part to be other than sober-minded, reverent toward truth and goodness, and responsive
to every high and holy appeal. A flippant,
frivolous, undevout poet is as abnormal as the
undevout astronomer, and, for the same reason,
that it is his special vocation to deal with what
is elevated and unearthly. Unnatural as it is
in the sphere of prose expression, it is far more
so in poetry, where, through the medium of the
imagination, the poet is supposed to soar beyond
all that is visible and material into the upper and
purer air of thought and truth and love and
beauty. It is to the lasting honor of American
letters that no one of her representative poets
has failed to meet these high conditions, even
Poe, with all his errors and weaknesses, holding
an exalted view of verse as the " rhythmical expression of beauty," and never condescending
for a moment to the rôle of the buffoon and
mountebank. By no one of our poets was this
high conception of verse more vigorously main-

tained than by Lowell, so that nothing more
surely provoked his righteous contempt than the
spectacle of one of these misguided poetasters
playing with his mission as a toy, utterly obli-
vious of the divine vocation to which he was
called.   Even in his humor he was serious, and
insisted that the man of letters as such should be
above the base and belittling, and dwell, as Milton dwelt, " in the quiet and still air of delightful
studies." Thus, in one of his sonnets, suggested
by the reading of the meditative Wordsworth,
he writes:

> " Far 'yond this narrow parapet of Time,
>   With eyes uplift, the poet's soul should look
>   Into the Endless Promise, nor should brook
>   One prying doubt to shake his faith sublime;
>   To him the earth is ever in her prime
>   And dewiness of morning; he can see
>   Good lying hid from all eternity,
>   Within the teeming womb of sin and crime;
>   His soul should not be cramped by any bar;
>   His nobleness should be so godlike high
>   That his least deed is perfect as a star,
>   His common look majestic as the sky,
>   And all o'erflooded with a light from far,
>   Undimmed by clouds of weak mortality."

This is the Lowellian view of verse, and toward this celestial ideal he looked and wrought.

In such poems as " The Cathedral " and " The
Vision of Sir Launfal," he made close approxi-
mation to its realization, while in the general
tenor of his lines he never forgot the special
sphere in which he was working, and the " great
cloud of witnesses " by which he " was compassed
about."

BAYARD TAYLOR.

Bayard Taylor

1825–1878.

CHAPTER EIGHTH.

BAYARD TAYLOR.

IT might seem at first a little strange that, in a survey of the more reflective American poets, the name of Taylor should be at all included. We think of him, most especially, as a writer of prose, in the province of fiction, journalism, travels, letters, and critical miscellany; as the author of " Hannah Thurston," of " Views Afoot," and " Studies in German Literature "; and yet even here we are at once impressed with the uniform gravity of bearing and style that he evinces, which characterizes him at once as a meditative writer. Turning to his verse, we are surprised, perhaps, at its variety and compass, as it appears in descriptive, lyric, dramatic, and didactic form—in every accepted form, indeed, save that of the distinctly epic. As early as 1844, before he had reached his majority, the first collection of his verse appeared. Other collections were prepared and published in due succession, such as " Rhymes of Travel," " A Book of Romances and Lyrics and Song," " Poems of the Orient," " Poems of Home and Travel," " Home Pastorals, Ballads, and Lyrics," with such separate poems as " Lars, a Pastoral of Norway," and " The Picture of St. John "; his " Local Idylls and Ballads of the Civil War " revealing the depth and intensity of his loyalty in the face of such strong inducements to surrender it.   No reader can run over this list of descriptive and idyllic verse without being impressed with its contemplative type and purpose, the didactic element in its best form being everywhere present.   It was this specific teaching quality that Taylor possessed and aimed to exhibit, so that, from first to last, he pens his poems not so much for the sake of penning them, or for any distinct artistic effect, as thereby to diffuse sound and wholesome principles, and advance the cause of truth.

His great work as a translator in rendering Goethe's " Faust " to English readers is developed along the same high line of serious endeavor, while his three more elaborate dramatic poems are characteristically ethical in theme, de-

velopment, and purpose. In a word, the verse
is essentially reflective, as much so, indeed, as
is that of any of his great contemporaries, and
so persuasively so as to make it unintelligible
to those who examine it from any other point
of view. With this didactic feature, moreover,
there is seen in all such a clear and emotive
quality that interest is added to instruction, and
all the finer feelings of the heart awakened.
Seldom has a poet succeeded in being at one
and the same time so serious and so attractive,
so that in such selections as " Lars " or " St.
John " or " Amram's Wooing " or the " Ode
to Shelley," deep emotion is under the safe re-
strictions of reason, and reason, under the more
genial and generous influence of feeling. Of the
first of his dramas, " The Masque of the Gods,"
the author tells us that his chief purpose is to
show " the gradual development of man's conception of God." Of the second one, " The
Prophet," he writes that he aims " to represent
phases of spiritual development and their external
results which are hardly possible in any other
country than ours "; while of the last and greatest drama, " Prince Deukalion," he states : " The
central design or germinal cause of the poem is

to picture forth the struggle of man to reach the highest, justest, happiest, and hence most perfect conditions of human life on this planet."

Nothing could more clearly evince the profoundly meditative temper of Taylor's mind and poetic work than this conception and elaboration of his three dramatic poems along semi-religious lines, and with reference to the great problems of human life and destiny.

In stating, by way of preface, the argument of this last work—" Prince Deukalion," he alludes to " the passing away of the classic faith and the emergence of Christianity," and predicts an " era of which no simply loving and believing creature of God can fail to discover the prophecy within his own nature."   He takes up in turn the sublime questions of God and truth and immortality, and seeks in poetic form to embody and express some of the soul's deepest yearnings. The closing lines, as spoken by Prometheus, are thus significant :

> " For Life, whose source not here began,
> Must fill the utmost sphere of Man,
> And, so expanding, lifted be
> Along the line of God's decree,
> To find in endless growth all good,
> In endless toil beatitude."

In seeking for specific evidences and examples of Taylor's more meditative verse, we turn from his dramatic lines to the various collections of his lyrics, and, first of all, to his " Poems of the Orient." " When I read these poems," writes Stoddard, " I think that Bayard Taylor has captured the poetic secret of the East as no English-writing poet but Byron has." The very name of the collection suggests their semi-religious and reflective character, being a counterpart in verse of his prose papers on Eastern lands and peoples. Some of the titles are as follows: " The Temptation of Hassan Ben Khaled," " Arab Prayer," " Amram's Wooing," " The Angel of Patience," " Bedouin Song," " The Birth of the Prophet," " The Arab to the Palm," " The Mystery," and " To the Nile." One of these poems, " The Shekh," from the Arabic, deserves citation in full:

> " Not a single star is twinkling
>   Through the wilderness of cloud;
>   On the mountain, in the darkness,
>   Stands the Shekh, and prays aloud:
>
> " ' God, who kindlest aspirations,
>   Kindlest hope the heart within,
>   God, who promisest Thy mercy,
>   Wiping out the debt of sin,

" ' God, protect me in the darkness,
    When the awful thunders roll :
Evil walks the world unsleeping,
    Evil sleeps within my soul.

" ' Keep my mind from every impulse
    Which from Thee may turn aside ;
Keep my heart from every passion
    By Thy breath unsanctified.

" ' God, preserve me from a spirit
    Which Thy knowledge cannot claim ;
From a knee that bendeth never
    In the worship of Thy name ;

" ' From a heart whose every feeling
    Is not wholly vowed to Thee ;
From an eye that, through its weeping,
    Thy compassion cannot see ;

" ' From a prayer that goes not upward
    In the darkness and the fear,
From the soul's impassioned center,
    Seeking access at Thy ear.

" ' When the night of evil threatens,
    Throw Thy shelter over me ;
Let my spirit feel Thy presence,
    And my days be full of Thee.' "

This reads almost like a hymn from Watts or
Heber, reverent, trustful, and tender, pervaded
by that spirit of the Orient which, with some
admixture of superstition and possible bigotry,
is yet worshipful and devout.

In moments of lighter and yet contemplative strain, he sings thus in his lines " In the Meadows " :

> " I lie in the summer meadows,
>   In the meadows all alone,
>   With the infinite sky above me,
>   And the sun on his midday throne.
>
> " The infinite bliss of Nature
>   I feel in every vein ;
>   The light and the life of summer
>   Blossom in heart and brain.
>
> " But, darker than any shadow
>   By thunder-clouds unfurled,
>   The awful truth arises,
>   That Death is in the world."

So, in the sonnet beginning ·

> " The soul goes forth, and finds no resting-place
>   On the wide breast of Life's unquiet sea
>   But in the heart of man."

So, in his " In Articulo Mortis," he writes in most emphatic protest against all popish proffer of pardon in the hour of direst need :

> " Nay, Priest! nay;
>   Stand not between me and the fading light
>   Of my last hour ; I know my soul is weighed
>   With many sins ; but even knowing this, . . .
>   I will not lean upon another's arm,

Or bid a human intercessor plead
My perilous cause; but I will stagger on
Beneath my sins unto the feet of God."

One of the closing poems of this collection, entitled " The Mid-watch," is unique in American verse, both in its title and its peculiar lyrical excellence:

" I pace the deck in the dead of night,
    When the moon and the starlight fail,
And the cordage creaks to the lazy swells,
    And heavily flaps the sail."

In fine, one scarcely knows the salient characteristics and innermost spirit of Taylor who has not read and re-read these lyrics of the Orient, in their picture of the weird and semi-historical life of Arab and Moor. As we read them, and become absorbed for the time in their teachings and spiritual temper, we forget that we are reading the lines of Taylor, the novelist and journalist and traveler and literary critic and acute Anglo-German author. We recall, however, the fact that he was constitutionally contemplative; that much of his travel was in the lands of the Orient; that his " Letters " to his wife and others are full of a deep and tender pathos; that his Teutonic studies and affinities

induced in him an **intellectual gravity** ; and that,
even in his work as a critic, he always discovered
and emphasized those underlying moral **convictions that** make authors and literatures **what
they are.** Thus interpreted, we **come at length
to** look in **his** verse **for** clear **indications of the
presence** of the meditative. **In his collection,
"Home** Pastorals, Ballads, Lyrics, and **Odes,"** the
somewhat severe sobriety **of the Orient poems
gives place to a more flexible and attractive expression** of feeling, **as he sings of "The Holly-
tree," "The** Burden **of the Day," "The Sun-**
shine of the **Gods," "In my** Vineyard," **and**
" The Guests at **Night." Thus, in "The Burden of the Day," we read :**

> " Who shall rise and cast away
> First, the burden of the day?
> Who assert his place, and teach
> Lighter labor, nobler speech,
> Standing firm, erect, and strong,
> Proud as freedom, free as song?
>
> .   .   .   .   .
>
> Higher paths there are to tread ;
> Fresher fields around us spread ;
> Other flames of sun and star
> Flash at hand and lure afar :
> Larger manhood might we share,
> Surer fortune, did we dare!"

Here we mark a **freer, fuller note, as if, in-**
deed, **from the impassioned pen of Whittier, as**
he pleads for **truth** and right.

So, in his " Casa Guidi Windows," he sings in
plaintive strain of Mrs. Browning:

> " The quiet brow; the face so frail and fair
>   For such a voice of song; the steady eye,
> Where shone **the** spirit fated to outwear
>   Its fragile house; and in her features lie
>   The soft half-shadows of her drifting hair."

So, of Bryant he beautifully sings:

> " For he, our earliest minstrel, fills
>   The land with echoes sweet and long,
> Gives language to her silent hills,
>   And bids her rivers move **to song.**

> " He sings of mountains and of streams,
>   Of storied field and haunted dale,
> Yet hears a voice through all his **dreams,**
>   Which says, ' The good **shall yet prevail.' "**

Of his " Gettysburg **Ode " suffice it to say that**
it is confessedly **one** of the few historic national
lyrics of English **verse, as** it closes so sublimely:

> " Take them, O God, our brave,
>   The glad fulfillers of Thy dread decree,
> Who grasped the sword for Peace, and smote to save,
>   And, dying here for Freedom, also died for Thee."

Thus the verse runs on in drama, description, narrative, pastoral, sonnet, and general lyric, and always marked by a kind of Senecan dignity and seriousness, well befitting the poet himself, the high themes he treated, and the final purpose of his writing.

It was, indeed, largely because of this governing desire as an author to be helpful in his authorship to those for whom he wrote, that he ever keeps above the lower level of the flippant and trivial, on the high plane of sober endeavor and a reverent study of God and man.

It is thus that Stedman writes so appreciatively of him: " To think of him is to recall a person larger in make and magnanimity than the common sort, a man of buoyancy, hopefulness, sweetness of temper, stainless in morals, and of an honesty so natural that he could not be surprised into an untruth or the commission of a mean act." " Life for me," says the poet himself, " is the making of all that is possible out of such powers as I may have."

The powers he had were of no inferior order. No American writer in prose or verse has devoted himself with more intensity of purpose to making the most and best of that which God

had given him, and these are the authors of
whom it may be said, as we read in Taylor's
" Bedouin Song," that they will live

" Till the sun grows cold,
And the stars are old,
And the leaves of the judgment-book unfold."

OLIVER WENDELL HOLMES.

.

Oliver Wendell Holmes.
1809-1894.

OLIVER WENDELL HOLMES.

IN such a writer and poet as Holmes it might
be argued, presumptively, that the reflective feature would be less prominent than in Bryant,
Emerson, Longfellow, Whittier, and Lowell,
while an historical examination of his verse fully
confirms this presupposition. The main currents of his mind set in other directions; his
prevailing themes were of a different order;
his literary ambitions, preferences, and purposes
were, in the main, different; so that his literary
constituency were led to expect from his pen
prose and verse in accordance with such a con-
stitutional bias. All this is true, and yet any
reader of Holmes fails to read his lines aright,
or to read aright between the lines, who fails to
find a meditative element fundamentally present and potent, not so conspicuous and demon-

139

strative as in other American poets, not so often seen, perhaps, but still existent and real, and all the more impressive, at times, by reason of its subdued and reserved character, and especially by reason of its close relation to other forms of verse so radically different. Nor is the explanation far to find: Holmes was a poet of man and human life; of the world about him and the world within him; and, hence, somewhat of the world above him; a poet of his own experience and of that of his fellows, in all the wealth and width of that experience; a versatile, many-sided delineator of human instincts, passions, and ideals, so that, in the nature of things, he must enter all avenues of lyric expression, strike all the chords of the heart of man, and treat of God and the world and human life and destiny. As he himself indicates, he has given us " Songs in Mahy Keys," singing now a note of gladness and now a note of more pensive tone, each heard in its fitting place and time, and together filling out the completed choral strain. Moreover, Holmes, as the son of Rev. Abiel Holmes, pastor of the Congregational Church at Cambridge, and author of " The Memoirs of the French Protestants," had an inherited tendency to the more devout and reflective side of verse; his voluntary passage from Congregationalism to Unitarianism being, as he conceived it, a transition from the narrower to the broader in matters of faith, giving him a wider range and larger liberty in the expression of his meditations on God and man. In his poem " The School-boy," as in his " Harvard Anniversary Poem of '86," he alludes to this change of front, the occasion of it, and its natural results. Whatever his doctrinal or denominational attitude, however, there was always a deep substratum of sober thought and life, revealing itself often when least anticipated, and, when expressed in unison with the lighter and more playful forms of verse, producing an effect altogether unique and impressive. A more specific inquiry as to the particular modes in which this contemplative element manifests itself will be of interest.

The poetry of Holmes in its entirety might be classified into three generic divisions, as national, humorous, and meditative, this last division being fully as characteristic as any, and expressed in various subordinate forms. As first in order, we note his " Hymns," which in themselves constitute a list of some dozen titles. Two of these are of special interest as included in our American hymnology for use in sacred worship. The one is called "A Hymn of Trust," as it reads:

> " O Love Divine, that stooped to share
>   Our sharpest pang, our bitterest tear,
>   On Thee we cast each earth-born care,
>   We smile at pain when Thou art near!"

The other is called "A Sun-day Hymn," as it reads:

> " Lord of all being! throned afar,
>   Thy glory flames from sun and star,
>   Center and soul of every sphere,
>   Yet to each loving heart how near!"

Each of these hymns, it is interesting to note, was published in " The Professor at the Break-fast-Table," " hymns," writes Duffield, " among our most acceptable and admirable Christian lyrics." It was in connection with the second of these lyrics that the author invited all his readers " to join in singing [inwardly] this hymn to the Source of the light we all need to lead us." Closely connected in spirit with these two selections is what is called " The Parting Hymn "

" Father of mercies, heavenly Friend,
We seek Thy gracious throne;
To Thee our faltering prayers ascend,
Our fainting hearts are known!"

So, the lyric entitled " The Army Hymn ":

" O Lord of hosts! almighty King!"

In addition are such as the " Hymn after the
Emancipation Proclamation," " Hymn for the
Fair at Chicago," " For the Dedication of Me-
morial Hall at Cambridge," " For the Laying
of the Corner-stone of Harvard Memorial Hall,"
" For the Two Hundredth Anniversary of
King's Chapel," " At the Dedication of the
Holmes Hospital at Hudson," " The Word of
Promise," " At the Funeral Services of Charles
Sumner," " For the Inauguration of the Statue
of Governor Andrew," and the " Hymn for the
Class-meeting," one of his choicest lyrics, as it
opens:

" Thou gracious Power, whose mercy lends
The light of home, the smile of friends,
Our gathered flock Thine arms infold
As in the peaceful days of old."

In fine, there are not a few of these poems,
under the title of songs, odes, tributes, and

sonnets, which in character and form are so
strictly reflective that they could safely be
classed under the division of hymns, surcharged
as they are with a kind of devotional and spiritual fervor.   In addition to hymns, there is a
second class of meditative poems that might be
termed " Verses for Occasions," written at the
time for special purposes, and embracing much
of that commemorative or reminiscent verse in
the composition of which Holmes was often at
his best.   Such are his loving tributes to the
great American authors and benefactors of his
time, in which he voices his own personal gratitude, and congratulates American letters and
the American people as the inheritors of their
fame.   Thus, in his poem " Bryant's Seventieth
Birthday," he sings in grateful strain :

> " This was the first sweet singer in the cage
> Of our close-woven life.   A new-born age
> Claims in his vesper song its heritage.
> How can we praise the verse whose music flows
> With solemn cadence and majestic close,
> Pure as the dew that filters through the rose?
> How shall we thank him that in evil days
> He faltered never ; nor for blame nor praise
> Nor time nor party shamed his earlier lays? "

So, in his lines to Longfellow :

" Ah, gentlest soul! how gracious, how benign
Breathes through our troubled life that voice of thine."

So, to Whittier, on his eightieth birthday, he writes in loving salutation, as also " In Memory of Lincoln,"and in sorrow for the smitten nation ·

" Dear Lord, with pitying eye behold
   This martyr generation,
Which Thou, through trials manifold,
   Art showing Thy salvation ;
Oh, let the blood by murder spilt
Wash out Thy stricken children's guilt
   And sanctify our nation!
Our hearts lie buried in the dust
   With him so true and tender,
The patriot's stay, the people's trust
   The shield of the offender ;
Yet every murmuring voice is still,
As, bowing to Thy sovereign will,
   Our best-loved we surrender."

Thus these memorial tributes continue, to Burns, to Garfield, Halleck, Everett, Moore, Lowell, Washington, Mrs. Stowe, and others, alternating between eulogy and elegy ; emphasizing the reflective and the pensive elements of life, and expressing in varied form many of the finest forms of idyllic verse. Nothing that Holmes has written, in prose or song, more clearly re-

veals his sensitive and affectionate nature, the
firm hold that he had upon the friends of his
earlier and middle life, and how easy it was for
him for the time being to subordinate the professor and the poet to the man and the friend.
So true is this that even in his national and humorous verse the more sedate and meditative
features of his character come into prominence,
as in " Old Ironsides," " Robinson of Leyden,"
" An Appeal for the Old South," " The Last
Charge," " God Save the Flag," and " A Voice
of the Loyal North."

By far the most extended list of his meditative poems, however, is found in those special
lyrics which have been well characterized as
" Poems of Moral and Spiritual Beauty," suffused with genuine sentiment, with a deep emotive and ethical purpose, and which, to the ob-
serving and sympathetic reader, unbosom, as
nothing else can, the innermost life and spirit of
the author.   Among these rich and choice selections any distinctions are almost invidious, so
uniform is their poetic merit and so high the
purpose that pervades them.   If forced to a discrimination we should cite the following : " Under the Violets," " The Crooked Foot-path,"

"The Voiceless," "Homesick in Heaven," "The Secret of the Stars," "Sun and Shadow," "The Last Look," "The Chambered Nautilus," "Our Limitations," "The Iron Gate," "The Living Temple," "A Mother's Secret," "An Old Year's Song," and "The Silent Melody."

From this rare anthology an occasional citation must suffice. Thus, in "The Voiceless":

> "Nay, grieve not for the dead alone,
> Whose song has told their heart's sad story;
> Weep for the voiceless, who have known
> The cross without the crown of glory!
> If singing breath or echoing chord
> To every hidden pang were given,
> What endless melodies were poured,
> As sad as earth, as sweet as heaven!"

In "Our Limitations" we read:

> "We trust and fear, we question and believe,
> From life's dark threads a trembling faith to weave.
> Eternal Truth! beyond our hopes and fears
> Sweep the vast orbits of Thy myriad spheres!"

So, in "The Iron Gate":

> "If word of mine another's gloom has brightened,
> Through my dumb lips the heaven-sent message came;
> If hand of mine another's task has lightened,
> It felt the guidance that it dares not claim."

In " The Living Temple " he sings, as a devout
Christian scientist and in loftiest strain :

> " Not in the world of light alone,
> Where God has built His blazing throne,
> Nor yet alone in earth below,
> With belted seas that come and go,
> And endless isles of sunlit green
> Is all thy Maker's glory seen ;
> Look in upon thy wondrous frame,
> Eternal wisdom still the same! . . .
> O Father! grant Thy love divine
> To make these mystic temples Thine!
> When wasting age and wearying strife
> Have sapped the leaning walls of life,
> When darkness gathers over all,
> And the last tottering pillars fall,
> Take the poor dust Thy mercy warms,
> And mold it into heavenly forms!"

Such are some examples of this wealth of
lyric verse on its contemplative side, expressing
some of the sweetest poetic sentiments that
Holmes has given us, and, even on the strictly
literary and artistic side, yielding not a whit to
anything that he has written. Readers of Holmes
who think of him as merely an after-dinner
poet or a maker of jolly rhymes for festivals
and class reunions, or as the author only of
" Aunt Tabitha," " Bill and Joe," and " The

Broomstick Train," quite mistake, after all, his
real temper and merit, and unwittingly lose a
large part of that personal satisfaction that comes
from a closer familiarity with his more subdued
and sensitive verse. And this leads us to note
that the great characteristic of his poetry as
meditative is its mental and moral wholesome-
ness; its soundness, sanity, and good sense; its
conspicuous freedom from the morose, ascetic,
and revolting; and from those one-sided and
hence defective views which mar the unity of so
many gifted authors in modern prose and verse.
Meditative verse, from its very etymology (*med-
itari*), means thoughtful verse, sentiment marked
by sense and some good degree of mental life,
while it is equally suggestive to note that the
word " meditation " is from the same verbal base
as *mederi*, meaning " to heal "; so that we have
here the two ideas of sanity and soundness,
thought in healthful forms, free from the morbid
and injurious, and directly contributive to the
best results in mind and character. A recent
writer in the " Forum " emphasizes the neces-
sity of a healthful tone in American Letters.
Whittier, in a review of Holmes's poems, pur-
posely speaks of mirth and medicine as a

happy combination illustrated in his verse.   In
no American or English bard have these two elements been so aptly conjoined, so that the sum-
total effect has been healing to the spirit, and
provocative of every wholesome impulse and
tendency.

In meditative verse such a characteristic is
especially notable and helpful, mainly because of
the comparative ease with which such a type
of verse degenerates into the unduly sedate and
serious.

Holmes has shown us most conclusively that
verse, because reflective, need not be revolting;
that sober suggestion may be couched in the
most attractive forms; that rational pleasantry
and good cheer have their appropriate place in
such an order of poetry, and that it is the envi-
able office of the lyrist, on the contemplative
side, to gladden, inspire, and encourage the human heart, and lift the life of his fellows toward
God and all that tends to goodness.

It is by the perusal of just such poetry as
this—true, tender, and ennobling—that many a
weary hour may be enlivened and enriched.

HARRIET BEECHER STOWE.

H. B. Stowe

1812–

HARRIET BEECHER STOWE.

" No one," writes Mr. Stedman, " can enter upon the most cursory review of our literature without being struck by the share which women have had in its production. A sisterhood of song has even in America a just and distinctive regard." To the same effect, and by way of prophecy, Professor Richardson writes: " There can be no question that the work of women in American literature is hereafter to command a study as deep as that bestowed upon the work of men." While we have no American authoress of the rank of Mrs. Browning in verse or George Eliot in fiction, we have in our earlier and developing literature a goodly number of women who have done and are doing a most commendable work in authorship, and so in-

155

creasingly distinctive as to demand the special
study of the critic.

If we inquire as to the particular provinces in
which our authoresses have done their best work,
we shall not find them, naturally, in the realm
of historical and philosophic criticism, nor, indeed, in that of epic and dramatic verse, but
rather in the wide departments of descriptive
miscellany, fiction, and lyric verse. It is significantly to the last of these departments, the lyric,
that our attention is directed, as illustrated in
such collections as Mrs. Sigourney's " Moral
Pieces in Prose and Verse " and Celia Thaxter's
" Driftweed." Still more to our purpose, it is
pertinent to state that it is, most of all, in the
domain of the meditative lyric that American
poetesses, as also British, have won distinction,
as there is no order of verse which, in its deep
and delicate sensibilities, is more thoroughly
germane to the nature and ideals of woman.
Emotional verse, especially in the line of the reflective and pensive, is her chosen sphere, and,
indeed, absolutely essential to the highest expression of her genius. Such a compend as the
recently prepared " Library of American Literature " or Griswold's " Female Poets of Amer-

ica" will furnish abundant examples illustrative of the character and spirit of our contemplative verse.

The names and poems of some of these lyrists may be cited and sufficient extracts quoted to give to the reader the desire to multiply them at pleasure. Thus from the pen of the gifted Celia Thaxter we note such a title as "The Watch of Boon Island," beginning:

> "They crossed the lonely and lamenting sea."

One of her poems, entitled "Song," is full of tender beauty:

> "We sail toward evening's lonely star
>   That trembles in the tender blue;
> One single cloud, a dusky bar,
>   Burnt with dull carmine through and through,
> Slow-smoldering in the summer sky,
>   Lies low along the fading west.
> How sweet to watch its splendors die,
>   Wave-cradled thus and wind-caressed!

> "How like a dream are earth and heaven,
>   Star-beam and darkness, sky and sea;
> Thy face, pale in the shadowy even,
>   Thy quiet eyes that gaze on me!
> Oh, realize the moment's charm,
>   Thou dearest! we are, at life's best,
> Folded in God's encircling arms,
>   Wave-cradled thus and wind-caressed."

Mrs. Louise Chandler Moulton makes selection almost invidious among such choice examples as " The House of Death," " To-night," and " We Lay Us Down to Sleep."   We quote from the last a stanza or two:

> " We lay us down to sleep,
>   And leave to God the rest,
> Whether to wake and weep
>   Or wake no more be best.

> " Some faithful friends we've found,
>   But they who love us best,
> When we are underground,
>   Will laugh on with the rest.

> " No task have we begun
>   But other hands can take ;
> No work beneath the sun
>   For which we need to wake."

Of similar reflective pathos and beauty are some of the lyrics of Mrs. Harriet Prescott Spofford, such as " A Sigh " and " Magdalen," " Fantasia, " and that exquisite production, " Music in the Night ":

> " When stars pursue their solemn flight,
>   Oft in the middle of the night
> A strain of music visits me,
> Hushed in a moment silverly

> Such rich and rapturous strains as make
> The very soul of silence ache
> With longing for the melody."

Mrs. Piatt's "Why Should We Care?" "Transfigured," and "His Share and Mine," are of the same deep and pensive pathos, breaking out at times into something like poetic passion.

> " If sand is in the South, frost in the North,
>   And sorrow everywhere and passionate yearning,
>   If stars fade from the skies, if men go forth
>   From their own thresholds and make no returning,
>   Why should we care? "

Mrs. Mary Mapes Dodge, in her "Two Mysteries," "The Stars," "Infoldings," and "Shadow Evidence," sounds the same subjective strain. Miss Phelps (Mrs. Ward), in her "Songs of the Silent World," has sounded as clear and sweet a note as any of her sex in this particular species of American lyrics, as in "An Autumn Violet" and other selections. So, in the deeply religious lines of the Carys, Alice and Phœbe, and of the Goodales, Elaine and Dora, poetic genius and art combine to furnish a well-nigh perfect product, as seen in such specimens as "Nearer Home," "Ashes of Roses," and "Eventide." Helen Jackson, in her "Resurgam," Mrs.

Sarah Orne Jewett, in " A Child's Grave,"
Emma Lazarus, in her lyrico-dramatic " Dance
to Death," and Miss Woolsey, in " Lohengrin,"
Miss Osgood, in " Driving Home the Cows,"Miss
Perry, in " Some Day of Days," Miss Smith, in
" Sometime," Miss Wilcox, in " Solitude," Miss
Bates, in " A Lament," Miss Clymer, in her
" Song," beginning:

> " Oh, trust me not unless thy soul
> Can claim my soul as thine,"

and similarly excellent specimens from the pens
of Miss Larcom, Miss Thomas, Mrs. Whitney,
Miss Coolbrith, and others, and a large and
worthy list of similarly gifted singers, are open
to the study of the lover of heartfelt verse expressed in finished form and taste.   It is only
when one begins to select from this list either as
to names or poems that he finds his difficulties
so increasing as to compel him to refer the reader
to his own intelligent judgment.   The marvel is
that Mr. Stedman and Miss Hutchinson, in their
" Library of American Literature," have evinced
such delicate wisdom in this regard, so as practically to meet the full purpose of their collection
and yet be true to the living and the dead.   Dif-

ficult as such a discrimination is with reference
to authors proper, it is preëminently so in regard
to that large and growing class of authoresses
whose special work and place so often put to the
extremest test the judgment of the critic.

There is one American authoress, however, of
so representative a reputation that she deserves
at our hands a separate study, in common with
the names of Lowell, Emerson, and Holmes.
The gifted daughter of a gifted father; a member
of a characteristic American family of national re-
pute, through the father and sons, in the American pulpit; the wife of a distinguished biblical
scholar and teacher; and possessed of a nature
constitutionally devout and earnest, it is but natural that we find her, both in prose and verse,
making valid contributions to serious and substantial literature. Penning in her girlhood a the-
sis on "The Immortality of the Soul," this meditative spirit evinced itself in such prose productions as "The Minister's Wooing," "Old Town
Folks," "Footsteps of the Master," "Bible
Heroines," and "House and Home Papers,"
to say nothing of "Dred," and her most notable
work, "Uncle Tom's Cabin," begotten as it was
out of her profound personal interest in the suf-

ferings of the oppressed. Never has a writer
undertaken and prosecuted literary work with a
more devout desire to realize the Baconian ideal,
" in the glory of God and the relief of man's
estate."   But we are writing of American meditative verse, and we turn at once to Mrs. Stowe's
" Religious Poems," her one most distinctive
contribution in this direction, and signally indic-
ative of her innermost religious spirit. Though
embodied in a single volume of but little more
than one hundred pages, they are replete with
beauty and literary interest, especially significant as coming from the writer of " Uncle Tom's
Cabin," and serving to confirm the same profound contemplative character that we discern in
her most secular prose. The titles of some of
the choicest of these religious lyrics are as follows : " St. Catharine Borne by Angels," " The
Other World," " The Inner Voice," " Abide in
Me and I in You," " Consolation," " Only a
Year," " Hours of the Night," with its seven separate poems, and " St. Peter's Church."   From
first to last these poems are idyllic, full of the
tenderest religious feeling, marked, above all, by
a pervading purpose to be of personal service
in them to those in need of sympathy, and re-

vealing, as nothing else she has written does, what her ideal of literature and life has been and how efficiently she has realized it.

In the first selection of the volume, " St. Catherine Borne by Angels," are some beautiful stanzas:

" Slow through the solemn air, in silence sailing,
　　Borne by mysterious angels, strong and fair,
　She sleeps at last, blest dreams her eyelids veiling,
　　Above this weary world of strife and care.

" So, o'er our hearts sometimes the sweet, sad story
　　Of suffering saints, borne homeward, crowned and blest,
　Shines down in stillness with a tender glory,
　　And makes a mirror there of breathless rest.

" For not alone in those old Eastern regions
　　Are Christ's beloved ones tried by cross and chain ;
　In many a home are His elect ones hidden,
　　His martyrs suffering in their patient pain."

So, in the exquisite poem " The Charmer," in which Christ is represented as the one for whom the pagan world was looking and ardently waiting :

" ' Where is that Charmer whom thou bidst us seek?
　　On what far shores may His sweet voice be heard?
　When shall these questions of our yearning souls
　　Be answered by the bright Eternal Word?'

" But years passed on ; and lo! the Charmer came,
  Pure, simple, sweet, as comes the silver dew,
  And the world knew Him not : He walked alone,
  Encircled only by His trusting few."

A similar Christian strain is heard in " Only
a Year," " The Old Psalm Tune," " The Other
World," and " The Inner Voice," in all of which
it is difficult to tell which is the more impressive,
the sweet and tender sentiment of the songs, or
the rich and rhythmic melody in which they are
written.

So, in that inimitable lyric of prayer, " Abide
in Me and I in You," as it opens

" That mystic word of Thine, O sovereign Lord,
  Is all too pure, too high, too deep, for me ;
  Weary of striving, and with longing faint,
  I breathe it back again in prayer to Thee."

In her serial poem " The Hours of the Night ;
or, Watches of Sorrow," passing from " Mid-
night," through the four hours to " Day Dawn,"
and closing with the poem, " When I Awake I
am Still With Thee," consolatory verse rises to
its highest and purest level, as we find it in the
best hymnology of the Christian church.

In fine, no reader of American verse, on its
meditative side, can be said to know it fully, and

no student of the life and writings of Mrs. Stowe can be said to know her fully and at her best, until he has read these uplifting religious lyrics. They remind us more directly of the tender sentiments of the English Bonar and Heber and Miss Havergal, and our American Palmer, and that delicately sensitive nature, the lamented Sidney Lanier, than of any others, and serve to add to Mrs. Stowe's reputation for intellectual vigor and creative literary genius the scarcely less important qualities of sensibility and grace and exquisite artistic taste.

Nor does American literature or any other literature suffer by the prominent presence of genuine feeling in its prose and verse. To the degree in which it is genuine, it is healthful and helpful, serving to give tone to thought to soften what would otherwise be harsh and rough, and to give to authorship that gentleness and mellowness that it so often needs. Here lies the mission of such an order of prose as that of Irving, and here, especially, lies the mission of lyric verse as distinct from the epic and dramatic, in maintaining what Disraeli has called "the Amenities of literature." When, moreover, these lyrics pass out of the strictly secular into the sphere of the subjective and even the sacred, as they do in the verse of Mrs. Stowe, and, to a great degree, in that of all the lyrists we have studied, then does poetic expression rise to its most attractive form, and take its place, as it rightly should, among the most beneficent ministries to men.

AMERICAN MEMORIAL LYRICS: ELEGIES.

AMERICAN MEMORIAL LYRICS: ELEGIES.

OF the various forms of meditative verse, the elegy, from its very nature and purpose, is the most distinctively so. In fact, this is its exclusive feature. The different classes of lyric poetry are sometimes viewed under the one title—odes. These are heroic or epic, as seen in the national sonnets of Wordsworth and Milton; humorous, as seen in Moore; amatory, as in Burns; pastoral, as in Ramsay and Shenstone; sacred, as seen in Christian hymnology; moral or devotional, as seen in Spenser's " Heavenly Love " and " Heavenly Beauty "; and elegiac. This final form, as stated, is the most specifically meditative. It is sometimes called the Mournful Ode, or the Memorial Ode, being specifically lyrical in that it embodies and aims to express

the deepest and tenderest feelings **of the**
human heart; while there are in **all** prominent
literatures many **poems** that are **not** properly
called **elegies**, in which, however, the elegiac
element and spirit are so pronounced as to give
them practically an elegiac effect. Readers are
familiar with the standard elegies of British
letters, **Tennyson's, In Memoriam,** Milton's
" **Lycidas,**" **Shelley's** " **Adonais,**" Gray's
"**Elegy Written in a Country Churchyard,**" and
Matthew Arnold's " Thyrsis," nearly all of which
could **strictly be called In Memoriams or com-**
memorative poems, tributes to the memory
of such cherished **friends as Arthur** Hallam,
Edward **King, the poet Keats, and** Arthur Hugh
Clough. As far back as Chaucer's " Booke of
the Duchesse," a tribute to Lady Blanche, and
Spenser's " **Astrophel,**" a tribute to Sir Philip
Sidney, we note this **memorial verse,** appearing
later in such poems as Dryden's " Heroic Stanzas " on **Cromwell,** Wordsworth's **lines,** " At the
Grave of **Burns,**" and Landor's **lines,** " On
Southey's **Death**"; while **many poems,** such as
Milton's " Il Penseroso " and **Hood's** " Death-
bed," have a definitely marked elegiac quality,
not to speak of those numerous sonnets, scattered

up and down the pages of English letters, which
may be said to possess more of this feature than
of any other.

In American letters the same literary laws
obtain, though on a narrower scale. We note
the same divisions of lyric verse, the same memorial spirit characterizing much of the poetry,
while, here and there, a separate elegy is found
possessed of special idyllic merit, and expressing
meditative sentiment on the side of grief. Naturally, in such a body of verse as the American,
this particular type of lyric cannot be expected
to be abundant or even singularly able. The
nation is as yet too young, the range and depth
of its experience too limited, the distinctive quality and aim of its civilization too material, for
its developing literature to express much of this
subjective spirit in its verse. Almost any kind
of lyric is more in keeping with the prevailing
impulses and the environment, while it is this
very fact that lends special significance to any
such meditative poetry that does exist, and in-
sures its fuller expression, as a form, in the future
history of the literature. Memorial tributes are
found, as far back as 1657, in " The Life and
Death of John Cotton," by John Norton ; in 1670,

in " The Life and Death of Richard Mather," by
Increase Mather; in 1678, in Nerton's " Funeral
Elegy upon Anne Broadstreet "; in 1685, in
Cotton Mather's quaint discourse, " An Elegy
on the Much-to-be-Deplored Death of that
Never-to-be-Forgotten Person, Rev. Mr. Na-
thaniel Collins "; until, in 1682, we note, by Cot-
ton Mather, " A Poem to the Memory of Hiram
Oakes "; in 1715, " A Poem on the Death of
Joseph Green," by Nicholas Noyes; in 1727,
"A Poem on the Death of George I.," by Mather
Byles; " An Elegy on the Death of Daniel Oliver," in 1732, by the same author, one of the
most prolific elegiac poets of the time; " An
Elegiac Poem on the Death of George Whitefield," by Phillis Wheatley Peters, in 1770; and so
on, through the eighteenth century, in the verse
of Brackenridge and Barlow, and closing with
Alsop's " Monody on the Death of Washington,"
in 1800—a collection of memorial literature,both
in prose and verse, whose merit is in the inverse
ratio of its amount, whose enforced reading
might have endangered the health of the heroes
it eulogizes, and whose record is important only
as showing the continuity of literary growth.
That the editors of the recently published

" Library of American Literature " patiently and
courageously traversed this wide waste of words,
and are still living and in good spirits, is proof
positive of what man and woman can endure.
Coming to the nineteenth century, a few of the
most notable of our American elegies may be
cited. In the verse of Poe there is a decided
elegiac tone and quality. In fact, it might be
said that, with some rare exceptions, as " El-
dorado " and " Eulalie," the poetry throughout
is pitched in the minor key, often breaking out
in a dirge or a despairing wail over the woes of
earth and the fate of man. Even of " The Bells "
the two longest stanzas sound this dire note,
beginning, respectively :

and
> " Hear the loud alarum bells,"
>
> " Hear the tolling of the bells."

The theme of his most celebrated poem, " The
Raven,"as he tells us, is that of " a lover lament-
ing his deceased mistress," a veritable elegy,
with its sad refrain of " nevermore." So, in his
poems " Lenore," " The Colosseum," "Annabel
Lee," " Ulalume," and briefer selections, there
is the same commemorative tenor and spirit over
something or some one lost.

Turning to Bryant, we note such elegiac poems
as " Blessed Are **They that Mourn**," beginning :

> " Oh, deem not they are blest alone
>   Whose lives a peaceful tenor keep ;
> The Power who pities man hath shown
>   A blessing for the eyes that weep."

So, his " Hymn to Death," " The Indian Girl's
Lament," " Rizpah," " The Old Man's Funeral,"
" The Two Graves," " The Living Lost," " The
Burial of Love," and his significant lines on " The
Death of Lincoln " :

> " Oh, slow to smite and swift to spare,
>   Gentle and merciful and just!
> Who, in the fear of God, didst bear
>   The sword of power, a nation's trust!
>
> " In sorrow by thy bier we stand
>   Amid the awe that hushes all,
> And speak the anguish of a land
>   That shook with horror at thy fall.
>
> " Thy task is done; the bond are free;
>   We bear thee to an honored grave,
> Whose proudest monument shall be
>   The broken fetters of the slave.
>
> " Pure was thy life; its bloody close
>   Hath placed thee with the sons of light,
> Among the noble host of those
>   Who perished in the cause of Right."

This noble eulogy and elegy is fitly followed by the poem " The Death of Slavery."

All readers have marked the meditative character of Bryant's verse, while it is here in place to note that this contemplative cast often appears in the elegiac form, as best expressive of the pensive habit of Bryant's mind. The same is true, approximately, of Emerson, in so far as the general character of his verse is concerned, while he has given us, in two or three instances, notable examples of the elegy proper, as in his " In Memoriam," written as a tribute to his brother Edward, as he sings in plaintive strain :

> " There is no record left on earth,
>   Save in tablets of the heart,
> Of the rich inherent worth,
>   Of the grace that on him shone."

So, in his " Dirge " :

> " But they are gone—the holy ones
>   Who trod with me this lovely vale ;
> The strong, star-bright companions
>   Are silent, low, and pale."

It is especially in his threnody over the death of his beloved and promising son that he unbosoms his soul in lines of tenderest grief :

"And, looking over the hills, I mourn
The darling who shall not return. . . .
The gracious boy, who did adorn
The world whereunto he was born;
I hearken for thy household cheer,
O eloquent child! . . .
The brook into the stream runs on,
But the deep-eyed boy is gone.
Was there no star that could be sent,
No watcher in the firmament,
No angel from the countless host
That borders round the crystal coast,
Could stoop to heal that only child,
Nature's sweet marvel undefiled,
And keep the blossom of the earth,
Which all her harvests were not worth?
O child of Paradise,
Boy who made dear his father's home,
In whose deep eyes
Men read the welfare of the times to come,
I am too much bereft."

Thus the lines run on in deep, pathetic flow, revealing, as nothing else does which Emerson has written, what a large and loving nature the great man had, and how little we know of authors until some bitter sorrow has sanctified their natures and opened up the well-springs of feeling and sympathy that hitherto have lain concealed. Bayard Taylor, in similar strain, wrote his elegy on the death of his beloved wife, Mary

Agnew. So, in Longfellow's verse, there is a decided elegiac element, appearing, partly, in such meditative poems as " The Reaper and the Flowers," "God's-Acre," " Resignation," " Suspiria," and " The Two Angels," and, also, in specific examples of memorial poetry, as his lines on " Charles Sumner " :

> " Garlands upon his grave
>   And flowers upon his hearse,
>   And to the tender heart and brave
>   The tribute of this verse.

> " His was the troubled life,
>   The conflict and the pain,
>   The grief, the bitterness of strife,
>   The honor without stain. . . .

> " Were a star quenched on high,
>   For ages would its light,
>   Still traveling downward from the sky,
>   Shine on our mortal sight.

> " So, when a great man dies,
>   For years beyond our ken
>   The light he leaves behind him lies
>   Upon the paths of men."

So that beautiful and touching elegy entitled " Three Friends of Mine," beginning :

> " When I remember them, those friends of mine,
>   Who are no longer here, the noble three
>   Who half my life were more than friends to me,
>   And whose discourse was like a generous wine."

So, most of all, in his " Morituri Salutamus," a
poem from which no one line can be spared,
filled to the full with tender lyric richness, replete with thought and love and faith and hope,
the inimitable model of all modern elegies, a
poem sufficient in itself to have made the name
of Longfellow great and dear for all time.

Turning to Whittier, the poet of trust and
cheer and simple, homely life, we find his pages
full of idyllic charm, characteristically reflective, and often marked by deep elegiac feeling.
Such poems are " The Female Martyr," " Telling the Bees," " The Swan Song of Parson
Avery," his tributes to Toussaint l'Ouver-
ture, to Garrison, Channing, Wordsworth,
Burns, and others. His poem " Ichabod," an
elegy on the lost reputation of Webster by
reason of his compromising attitude toward the
fugitive-slave law, is one of painful interest, as
he writes:

> " So fallen! so lost! the light withdrawn
>   Which once he wore!
>   The glory from his gray hairs gone
>   Forevermore!"

In " The Lost Occasion," written thirty years
later, he continues the elegiac lament over the

fallen hero in that he did not live to see the final triumph of justice in the outcome of the Civil War, the emancipation of the slave.

One of the four volumes of Whittier's most recently published verse is entitled "Poems Reminiscent and Religious." This is but another name for meditative verse, in which the elegiac feature is also prominent, as in "Memories," a sweet testimonial to a "beautiful and happy girl" of his youth, and in "My Trust," touching lines to the memory of his mother:

> "A picture memory brings to me:
> I look across the years to see
> Myself beside my mother's knee;
> I wait in His good time to see
> That, as my mother dealt with me,
> So with His children dealeth He."

In such poems as "At Last," "What the Traveler Said at Sunset," and "The Light that is Felt," who can discern the dividing line between the contemplative and the prophetic, as, with his eye both on earth and heaven, he is rapidly preparing for the peace of God that just awaits him, and has already been granted him!

Turning to the poetry of Lowell, it is significant to note that it opens with his "Threnodia":

> " Gone, gone from us! and shall we see
> Those sibyl-leaves of **destiny,**
>   Those calm eyes, nevermore? "

Of a similar **spirit** is his sonnet " To the Spirit
of **Keats,"** and his tender poem " On the Death
of a Friend's Child," in which we read the suggestive lines :

> " 'Tis sorrow builds the shining ladder up,
> Whose golden rounds are our calamities,
> Whereon our firm feet planting, nearer God
> The spirit climbs, and hath its eyes unsealed.
> True is it that Death's face seems stern and cold,
> When he is sent to summon those we love ;
> But all God's angels come to us disguised :
> Sorrow and sickness, poverty and death,
> One after other lift their frowning masks,
> And we behold the seraph's face beneath,
> All radiant with the glory and the calm
> Of having looked upon the front of God."

So, his poems " She **Came and Went** " and
" The Changeling," his memorial **verses to**
Kossuth, Garrison, Channing, Hood, and others,
" Auf Wiedersehen," " After **the** Burial," and
" The First **Snowfall,"** in which he sings of his
lost child

> " I thought of a mound in sweet Auburn,
> Where a little headstone stood. "

His three notable memorial poems, " The Fight at Concord Bridge," " Under the Old Elm," and "An Ode for the Fourth of July," are national in character and purpose, though reminiscent and reflective. Thus, from first to last, through the record of our American verse this meditative and memorial strain is heard, sometimes in the quiet and subdued notes of contemplation, and often in the deep and passionate cry of sorrow over the irreparable losses of earth. Moreover, it may be said that, with the single exception of the hopeless key to which the verse of Poe is tuned, these poetic sentiments are hallowed and glorified by the presence of Christian hope and trust. Even in so rollicking and humorous a poet as Holmes, rare examples of the reflective and commemorative are found, while in such poets as Willis and the sisters Cary and Mrs. Stowe the secular passes into the scriptural and spiritual, and the contemplative into the devotional and religious; eulogy and elegy combine, and the final effect of the verse, as a whole, is to ennoble and subdue the hearts of those who read it with anything like an appreciative sympathy.

AMERICAN DEVOTIONAL LYRICS: HYMNS.

AMERICAN DEVOTIONAL LYRICS: HYMNS.

ACCORDING to that division of lyric verse by which all its forms are included under the one title of odes, the most natural and complete classification of the odes would be that of secular and sacred, this last order being divisible into inspired or biblical, religious or spiritual, and moral or ethical. It is in this second collection of odes, the religious, that the hymns of the Christian church belong, midway between the inspired productions of Hebrew verse and the ethical poems of Wordsworth and Spenser and kindred authors. Each of these orders is distinctly meditative, while it is reserved for religious odes, as expressed in hymns, to embody this reflective element in some of the most devout and impressive forms known to literature.

Moreover, it may be said that American hymnology, as distinct from British, has had an in-
creasingly creditable history from the beginning.
This history opens, in 1640, with the publication
of the now celebrated " Bay Psalm-book," believed, on good authority, to have been the first
book printed in America, by the first printing-
press in America, in Cambridge, in the house
of Rev. Henry Dunster, the first president of
Harvard, who was chosen afterward to issue the
version in a revised and more acceptable form.
As the title indicates, it was exclusively a psalter,
" the whole Book of Psalms faithfully translated
into English meter." Then followed various collections, such as that of Sternhold and Hopkins,
1693 ; of Tate and Brady, 1741 ; Watts's Hymns,
1741 ; Nettleton's " Village Hymns," 1824 ;
" Songs by the Way," 1824, by Bishop Doane ;
Bishop Coxe's " Christian Ballads," 1840 ;
Hastings's "Devotional Hymns," 1815 , Palmer's
"Hymns and Sacred Pieces," 1865 ; Mrs. Stowe's
"Religious Poems," 1867 ; Phœbe Cary's "Poems
of Faith, Hope, and Love," 1868. The list of
what may be called denominational hymnals is
well-nigh limitless, and need not here be cited.

A question of special interest arises here as

to our American hymnists, who they are, in the main, and what classes of the community they mainly represent. The large majority of them belong to the clergy, with a goodly number from our distinctively literary men and women, authors by profession.

As to the first of these orders, the clergy, one is impressed by their prominence along this line if he will turn to the index of names in such a compilation as Duffield's " English Hymns," in which we have a list given us of our American hymn-writers from 1640 to 1850. So conspicuous is the abbreviation " Rev." in these columns that it first catches the eye and commands the attention. Beginning with the " Bay Psalm-book," its three editors, Welde, Richard Mather, and Eliot, "the apostle to the Indians," were clergymen. Following the list as it runs, we note the names of Cotton Mather, Nettleton, Judson, Leonard, Bacon, James Waddell Alexander, Bethune, Hedge, Hatfield, Palmer, Joseph Addison Alexander, Robinson, and others. Of bishops there is a notable list, as seen in Onderdonk, Whittingham, Bergen, Coxe, Huntington, and Doane. Not a few of these devotional authors have been college presidents, as

Dunster of Harvard, Davies of Princeton, " the earliest American hymnist," and Timothy Dwight of Yale, one of the revisers of Watts's collection. In this worthy work the Unitarian church has had a large and useful place, as seen in the hymns of Clarke and Hedge, Furness, Ware, Higginson, and Samuel Longfellow. In fine, American hymnology, as a species of meditative verse, has had from the outset this ministerial origin and impress, nor is it at all unnatural. Just because these lyrics are semi-scriptural and religious, born out of a definite Christian experience, and written on behalf of character and personal piety, are they germane to clerical habit, thought, and purpose. Who knows, indeed, but that in some instances more decided Christian results have been reached by some of the hymns of these preachers and teachers than by all the sermons and lectures they have delivered! while the history of our hymnology is thus happily connected with that of the American church and the American college. What better work did President Dunster ever do than to put the " Bay Psalm-book " into such form as to make it the acceptable version throughout the colonial era! The fact that Dwight's revision of Watts was

adopted not only **by** Congregationalists, **but**
by the Presbyterian General Assembly of 1800,
clearly shows its value. Who can compute the
sacred influence of Muhlenberg's " I would not
live **alway**," or of Bethune's " **It is not** death
to die," or of any one of a score of Ray Palmer's
religious lyrics that might be cited!

How much hymnal theology there is in the
Christian church ; substantial, evangelical doctrine, presented through the medium of the **devout** and **tender lyric, and thus** all the **more**
designed **to** reach the head through the heart!
All bigotry and even denominational difference
vanishes under the hallowed and fusing influence
of these sacred songs. The debates and nice
distinctions of the schools of divinity disappear
when the people of **God** in the unity and **com-**
munity of a simple faith come **together** in a service of song to unbosom the deepest **yearnings**
of the human **heart. All Protestants are then**
one great religious order, while even Protestants
and Romanists may find common ground in the
great Latin hymns of the older church. We have
yet to learn what a safe guide the heart is, after
all, in matters of faith and Christian doctrine.

The second class of prominence in the production of our hymns we find in our specifically literary men and women as a distinct order, writers by profession and preference, the standard names in American letters. To many of these as hymnists reference has already been made—to Whittier, Holmes, and Mrs. Stowe. An early and most fitting illustration of this type of lyrist is William Cullen Bryant, the author of no less than twenty hymns, such as "O Thou whose love can ne'er forget," "Deem not that they are blessed alone," "All praise to Him of Nazareth," "Go forth, O word of Christ, go forth," and the characteristic dedicatory quatrain:

> "O Thou whose own vast temple stands,
>   Built over earth and sea,
>   Accept the walls that human hands
>   Have raised to worship Thee."

So, from Mrs. Sigourney, the hymn "Onward, onward, men of heaven"; from Phœbe Cary, the lines, "One sweetly solemn thought" and the lyric "Nearer Home," and, from her sister, Alice, various lines of similar spirit.

As mentioned in discussing the meditative verse of such poets as Emerson, Longfellow, and Lowell, the dividing line between the moral poem, so-called, and the religious poem or hymn is so delicate as scarcely to be discernible. Nor is the emphasis here to be laid, as to the work of our best authors in the line of hymnology, on the amount of such verse that they have composed. This, as compared with that of the clergy, is limited indeed. The fact of interest is that our standard authors should have written any poems of this specific order, evincing thus the best features of their personal characters, their sympathy with the existence and mission of the Christian church, and their effort to minimize, as far as possible, the distance in American verse between the secular and the sacred.

Here again, however, the production of such a species of verse by standard secular writers is not unnatural, in that poetry, in its best forms, is the most fitting expression of the deeper and finer sensibilities, of hope and love and joy and trust, the utterance of genuine feeling, cultivated taste, and of imagination in its loftiest and purest exercise. As in British letters the sacred verse of Milton, Addison, Pope, and Cowper is a normal form of poetic utterance, so, when our representative American poets enter the domain of the religious lyric, they but add another evidence

of their genuine gift and mission **as poets.** In
this **high sense,** a hymn from Holmes or Whittier is as appropriate as when **it comes from the**
pen of Hastings or **Palmer.** Just here it **is in**
place to state that, as we have in English and
classical literature debates and orations that were
never pronounced in public, **so** may we expect
to find, and do find, **some of** these sacred lyrics
which have been composed with **no reference**
whatever to their use in the exercises of **Christian**
worship, but simply as one of the types in which
poetic genius embodies itself, composed **as liter-**
ature, and **not specifically as religious literature.**
Thus Whittier **wrote his lyrics " The Eternal**
Goodness " and " Our Master," which, **though**
not written as hymns, **may be** so used if need
be. Thus Holmes and Bryant and Lowell **wrote**
reflective verse as **verse, but so imbued** with
moral and spiritual life as to make it serviceable
in the rites of the church. **In this way, what**
Brookes calls " the theology of **the** English poets "
has been made an essential **and** attractive **part**
of English literature.

So, on the other hand, hymns as such **should**
possess some distinctive literary **character,**
should have an artistic as well as a religious

quality, and should be in good taste from an esthetic point of view, so as to commend themselves
to all students of form and lovers of literary art.
The violation of this principle is far too frequent,
so frequent as to have brought the whole de-
partment of hymnology into peril at the hands
of literary critics. The mere fact that such lyrics
are composed for the service of the church and
the needs of the common people does not, in
their judgment, justify the absence of definite
artistic excellence. Readers of taste are often
pained by these unliterary and non-literary ef-
fusions that are found in our collections and pass
for sacred poetry. In no sense known to criticism can they be called poetry, and should not
as such be imposed upon the acceptance of wor-
shipers. It is, indeed, because of the presumable
literary ignorance of the people as a whole that
they are thus imposed, devoid as they are both
of the structure and spirit of genuine verse, ill-
conceived and ill-expressed, and worthy of the
name of verse only in the sense that the lines
are metrical. It is needless to say that much of
the hymnology in use by the modern lay evan-
gelist is greatly at fault in this particular, a mere
jingle and doggerel and trick of words, as illiter-

ate and unpoetic as verse could well be and be verse at all. It cannot be wondered at that such an order of sacred song should offend the cultivated taste of literary men, and estrange them permanently from the ordinances of the church. The comparison of these productions with such a lyric as Milton's ode " On the Morning of Christ's Nativity," or Heber's "Epiphany Hymn," or the sacred oratorios of Handel and Mendelssohn, will indicate the difference between unliterary and literary hymnology.

Outside the two classes of hymnists mentioned, the clergy and the literati, it is interesting to note the origin of some of our religious poems from other sources, professional and non-professional—some of them, indeed, from obscure and unknown sources. President John Quincy Adams composed a number of hymns, as found in Lunt's " Christian Psalter." Dr. Abraham Coles, in his admirable version of " Dies Irae," has worked along the same lyric line. Examples of hymns whose authors are but little known are seen in such opening lines as

> " Oh, could I find from day to day
> A nearness to my God!"

written by Benjamin Cleveland;

" There is an hour of **peaceful rest,**"

by Tappan;

" I love to steal awhile away,"

by Mrs. Brown;

" Humbly before Thine awful throne,"

by Hillhouse; and others of equal excellence
by equally unknown authors, the same principle
being even more largely illustrated in British
verse. The beautiful patriotic lyric " God bless
our native land," so finely combining Christian truth and national good, and written by John
S. Dwight, son of President Dwight, is none the
less excellent because the reputation of the son
was overshadowed by that of the father. The
enjoyment of such literary work as " The Letters of Junius " or " The Imitation of Christ " is
not dependent upon the settlement of the dis-
puted question of their authorship.

A closing thought is in place, drawn from the
Greek etymology of our word " hymn," from
umnos, " a song," " a festive poem." The idea
of cheerful praise is a prominent one in the
root meaning, as also in that of " psalm," and, in
the Christian sense, cannot be too pronounced.
Meditative verse, as embodied in hymns, need

not thereby be unduly sedate, and, least of all,
mournful and morose, but find its best and
most natural expression in happy, hopeful sentiment. Memorial hymns there must be, hymns
adapted to times of trial and struggle, penitential
hymns, hymns of humiliation and spiritual mis-
giving, hymns of consecration, and such as set
forth in poetic form the cardinal doctrines of the
church. These have their place, but a compar-
atively limited place, in any properly conducted
Christian anthology. Etymologically and spiritually, the prime purpose of the hymn and psalm
is praise, as uttering the various emotions of
gratitude and hope and joy and adoration—
praise for common and special mercies, praise
for divine grace in all its manifold ministries to
the soul, the very word "praise" radically de-
noting the payment of a tribute to the source of
blessing. Hence the fitness of the Hallelujahs
of our Christian hymnology: "Praise ye Jeho-
vah" is the appropriate refrain of the religious
lyric. Wisely, indeed, was good Bishop Ken
guided by the grace of God and his own poetic
genius when he thus gave us the "Te Deum
Laudamus" of the Protestant church in his inspired doxology:

"Praise God, from whom all blessings flow."

SOME LATER LYRISTS.

197

SOME LATER LYRISTS.

WHEN we pass from the earlier representative poetry of America to the subsequent and closing decades of the century, we pass by no means from lyric verse of a high order of merit to that of mediocrity. The great writers of idyllic song have gone, in the death of Whittier and Lowell and their inimitable fellow-craftsmen, and yet the volume of such verse is ever enlarging before us, while, here and there, in "the choir at large," is heard a voice that seems to have caught somewhat of the art of the older bards, so that we are led to hope that the day of poetic power has not altogether passed away. It is as satisfactory as it is surprising and even anomalous to note that a nation as young as ours, and as commercial in its instincts and ambitions, should exhibit, from age to age through its literary history, so pronounced a development along the lines of lyric expression, and, most of all, on its contemplative side. Rich as our anthology is, and, naturally so, in lyrics of adventure and civic interest, of bold and martial ardor and of passionate outbursts on the rights and the wrongs of man, it is far richer in that subdued and more subjective order of ode and sonnet to which these pages have referred. Even close upon the ending of the Civil War this meditative type asserted its presence, and patriotic devotion embodied its feeling as much in the quiet expression of national losses and trials as in the more demonstrative expression of national triumph. The verses of our poets at the completion of our first century as a republic are marked by the same reflective comment on the past and present of the nation's history, while the ever-increasing tide of materialism in philosophy and trade has not, as yet, been able to quench, in any valid sense, this steady expression of the sentiments of the heart.

A passing reference to some of these later and living lyric bards is all that can be attempted, the name of Sidney Lanier recalling a life whose end seemed to be so untimely, and whose rich

introspective verse was so full of poetic promise.
John James Piatt, in his " Idyls and Lyrics of
the Ohio Valley " and " Poems of House and
Home," is a name to be remembered, such poems
as " The Morning Street," "A Lost Graveyard,"
"Apart," and " Leaves at My Window," indicat-
ing the reflective quality. William Winter, in his
lines on " An Empty Heart " and " Constance,"
strikes the same minor key, especially touching
in the tribute to Poe :

> " He was the voice of beauty and of woe,
>   Passion and mystery and the dread unknown ;
> Pure as the mountains of perpetual snow,
>   Cold as the icy winds that round them moan,
> Dark as the cave wherein earth's thunders groan,
>   Wild as the tempests of the upper sky,
> Sweet as the faint, far-off celestial tone
>   Of angel whispers, fluttering from on high,
>   And tender as love's tears when youth and beauty die."

Thomas Bailey Aldrich, in his verse throughout, reveals a high order of genius along this
special idyllic line, so that one is in serious doubt
as to what selections to emphasize among such as
" Flower and Thorn," " An Untimely Thought,"
" An Old Castle," " Prescience," and " Sleep,"
this last sonnet reading thus sweetly :

" When to soft sleep we give **ourselves away,**
And **in a** dream, as **in** a fairy bark,
Drift on and on through the enchanted dark
To purple daybreak, little thought we pay
To that sweet, better world we know by day;
We are clean quit of **it, as is a lark**
So high in heaven no human **eye** can mark
The thin, swift pinion cleaving through the gray.
Till we awake ill fate can do no ill,
The resting heart shall not take up again
The heavy load that yet must make it bleed;
For this brief space the loud world's voice is still,
No faintest echo of it brings us pain.
How will it be when we shall sleep indeed? "

This is the very perfection of lyric verse in its
more subdued and gentle forms, where thought
and feeling and taste and rhythmic art so combine as to leave nothing wanting in the final
impression of the poem.

So, Howells and Maurice Thompson, **Richard
Henry Stoddard,** Boner, and Cheney, **in his "A
Saint of Yore,"** have done noteworthy work as
poets in meditative miscellany.   **R. W.** Gilder,
in **" The New Day "** and other collections, **has**
given us some of the most **exquisite verse** of **the**
time in such examples as "The Celestial Passion,"
" A Christmas Hymn," and " Sonnet," while
the masterly American critic, Stedman, **has**

added to all his other estimable work his " Lyrics
and Idyls," so marked by classical correctness
and genuine poetic sentiment.

No one of our living lyrists has done more representative work along these special lines than
has Mr. Stedman. We have but to glance down
the list of his themes in verse to note the emphatic
presence of this chaste idyllic quality on the
side of reflection. Such are the poems " Too
Late," " The Protest of Faith," " Hope De-
ferred," " A Mother's Picture," " The Old
Love and the New," " At Twilight," " Darkness and Shadow," " The Sad Bridal," and
" The Ordeal by Fire," which last poem, had we
space, might be quoted in its entirety as illustrative of a profound and tender meditative-
ness. His justly celebrated " Dartmouth Ode,"
in its ten separate sections, is full of this quiet
charm of spirit and manner, as he recounts the
trials and triumphs, the hopes and disappoint-
ments, of youth. Thus, in the sixth section,
" Youth and Age," he sings in sweet and sober
strain :

> " How slow, how sure, how swift
> The sands within each glass ;
> The brief, illusive moments pass ;
> Half unawares we mark their drift,

Till the awakened heart cries out, 'Alas,
Alas! the fair occasion fled,
The precious chance to action all unused! '
And murmurs in its depths the old refrain,
' Had we but known betimes what now we know in vain!'"

So, in the beautiful reverie "The Undiscovered Country":

> " Could we but know
> The land that ends our dark, uncertain travel,
> Where lie those happier hills and meadows low,—
> Ah, if beyond the spirit's inmost cavil,
> Aught of that country could we surely know,
> Who would not go!"

Here is heard the voice of one of the new masters, if not of the old—a clear, hopeful, and an inspiring voice; and he who heeds it and follows it will rise at once to noble endeavor and wider outlook.

So have our departed lyrists sung, and so are singing those who still are among us; while the poverty of American letters in epic and dramatic verse finds its partial compensation in this wealth of reflective lyric product.

In fine, no literature of note has a richer record of lyric verse within the compass of a century, while no element of our developing poetic

life is fuller of promise than this as to the excellence and permanence of our literary work.
American literature has few great poets and
few great poems. It has, however, a large
amount of poetry that is thoroughly good—
characterized by faith in God and faith in man,
by faith in truth and right and love and spiritual law, and ministrant thereby to human life in
its daily and deepest needs.

www.ingramcontent.com/pod-product-compliance
Lightning Source LLC
Chambersburg PA
CBHW030831270326
41928CB00007B/995